Twayne's English Authors Series

Sylvia E. Bowman, *Editor*

INDIANA UNIVERSITY

Robert Louis Stevenson

 167

Robert Louis Stevenson

Robert Louis Stevenson

By IRVING S. SAPOSNIK

Haifa University

TWAYNE PUBLISHERS

A DIVISION OF G. K. HALL & CO., BOSTON

To Francie and her Offspring
No finer gift has man been given

Contents

Preface

Robert Louis Stevenson would have been the first to appreciate the impetus behind the writing of this book. Several years ago, when my intentions were mired in the limbo of inertia, a casual conversation produced the brute circumstance that prompted action. As I bemoaned the lack of valuable Stevenson criticism, I was persuaded to write a book to fill the void, a book comprehensive in its approach and balanced in its evaluation which would, above all, make people read Stevenson. The result follows.

There has not been a critical study of all of Stevenson's literature since Frank Swinnerton's (1914); and, although Swinnerton touches upon the several forms in which Stevenson wrote, he does not present a balanced picture of either the man or his work. More recently, the critical studies by Robert Kiely (1964) and Edwin Eigner (1966), while more accurate in their assessments, are somewhat restricted by their specialized format. My hope for the present book goes beyond all three.

As the first comprehensive study of Stevenson's work in more than fifty years, it is written to serve as an introduction to his literature; and it is free of bias, of special pleading, of any criteria beyond the literary. After the introductory biographical sketch (Chapter I), each chapter presents a discussion of a particular literary form which Stevenson employed. As the discussion proceeds from essay to novel, it reveals the many dimensions of a short but full literary career, a versatility rarely equaled among the Victorians. Yet it also reveals a writer not always equal to his intentions. Stevenson knew his deficiencies; in fact, he often paraded them self-consciously; and, if he is to stand as an imaginative though not always successful writer, he must do so on his own spindly but unshakeable legs.

Men, however, can stand alone far better than books about them. The present book emerges from years of graduate-student groping and careful nurturing by teachers who gave of themselves and their knowledge. First among these is John Jordan who gave more than the conventional guidance of a dissertation director. My students and colleagues at Wisconsin were likewise helpful. I owe a special debt of gratitude to my students in the Stevenson seminar who helped me test many of my assumptions and allowed me the luxury of believing that in most instances I was right, particularly Richard Sindel, who offered many valuable suggestions and endured several readings of the manuscript in its earliest and roughest stages. Among my colleagues, Karl Kroeber and Barton Friedman not only read the manuscript with a practiced eye but extended friendship and support.

In addition, I am grateful to those institutions—The American Philosophical Society and the Graduate School of the University of Wisconsin—who knew nothing of me as a person but were willing to extend financial aid because they had confidence in my work, and to those people, family and friends, who knew less about my work than about the person behind it and were yet willing to humor a quixotic pursuit of a critical El Dorado. Among these, my mother and grandmother stand out appropriately and deservedly, and also my uncle, Morris Yellin, who has been more than an uncle and often more than a father.

Finally, I would like to thank the Edinburgh Public Library, the Beinecke Library of Yale University, and Mr. Nigel Henley for permission to quote from unpublished Stevenson and Henley material.

IRVING S. SAPOSNIK

Haifa, Israel

Chronology

1850 Robert Louis Stevenson born, November 13, 8 Howard Place, Edinburgh.

1867 Enters Edinburgh University.

1871 Gives up engineering for law.

1872 Passes preliminary examinations for the Scottish bar.

1873 Meets Fanny Sitwell.

1875 Meets William Ernest Henley in Edinburgh Infirmary. Visits art colonies at Grez and Fontainebleu where he meets Fanny Osbourne. Admitted to Scottish bar.

1876 Canoe trip down the Oise River.

1878 Fanny Osbourne returns to America. Walking trip through the Cevennes. *An Inland Voyage; Picturesque Notes on Edinburgh.*

1879 Writes *Deacon Brodie* with Henley. Leaves for America. In Monterey, California, with Fanny Osbourne and her family. *Travels With a Donkey.*

1880 Lives in San Francisco; Fanny, in Oakland. Married in May; honeymoon at Silverado. Returns to England in August.

1881 Davos, Switzerland. Meets John Addington Symonds. *Virginibus Puerisque.*

1882 Lives in the south of France. *Familiar Studies of Men and Books; New Arabian Nights.*

1883 Hyères. *The Silverado Squatters; Treasure Island.*

1884 Leaves Hyères for Bournemouth.

1885 "Skerryvore," Bournemouth. Writes remaining plays with Henley. *A Child's Garden of Verses; More New Arabian Nights; Prince Otto.*

1886 *Dr. Jekyll and Mr. Hyde, Kidnapped.*

1887 Death of Thomas Stevenson. Stevenson sails for America, arrives New York City, September 7. Settles at Saranac. *Underwoods, Memories and Portraits.*

1888   Fanny leaves for California to find yacht. Letter from Henley sparks their quarrel. Stevenson sails for the South Seas aboard the yacht *Casco*. First cruise: The Marquesas, The Paumotus, The Society Islands, Hawaii.

1889   Leaves Honolulu aboard the *Equator* on second cruise. Purchases estate in Samoa. *The Wrong Box; The Master of Ballantrae.*

1890   Third cruise aboard *Janet Nicoll*. Settles in Samoa.

1891   *Ballads.*

1892   *Across the Plains; A Footnote to History.*

1893   Fanny's nervous breakdown. *Island Nights' Entertainments; Catriona.*

1894   Stevenson dies, December 3. *The Ebb-Tide.*

CHAPTER 1

The Light-Keeper

THE fascination of Robert Louis Stevenson's life has so enchanted his readers that they have often been unable to consider his literature apart from his life. As his reputation grew in the 1880's and 1890's, he was admired as much for his personal adventure as for his adventure fiction. Perhaps for no writer, therefore, is it as important to distinguish between life and biography. The first is factual, a series of events which can be summarized with at least chronological accuracy (see Chronology); the second, however, is the product of a fiction so elaborate that Stevenson indeed might have admired its ingenuity while he undoubtedly would have regretted its falsity.[1]

Unfortunately, most readers know the fabrication. In this version, best represented by Graham Balfour's official biography, Stevenson is very much the "Seraph in Chocolate," that effigy of a man that William Ernest Henley accused his protectors of manufacturing.[2] Most books written after Balfour's (1901) have attempted either to elaborate upon his misrepresentations or have assumed that the true Stevenson must be exactly the opposite of his caricature. The debunkers follow their own peculiar logic: for Balfour's effeminate *poseur,* they substitute an insatiable satyr who delights in his Robert-Burns-like quest for sexual satisfaction. Accordingly, to struggle through the Stevenson biographies is to arrive at an inescapable conclusion: by an inadvertent irony, the pattern of his biographies follows the circular structure of his fiction; although the action progresses, essential questions remain unresolved.

The details, even when unadorned, are not always clear. Born at midcentury to a comfortable Scottish family of engineers best known for their work with lighthouses, Stevenson endured a middle-class upbringing among the solemn surroundings of his Edinburgh homes—8 Howard Place where he was born, and 17

Heriot Row to which his family moved when he was six, hoping thereby to avoid the nagging illness which eventually forced him to leave Europe forever. An only child, he was troubled by his loneliness; and his isolation, together with his frequent illness, allowed his impressionable mind to dwell upon imagined horrors as both a threat and a relief. His chief aid in these excursions into fantasy was his nursemaid, Alison Cunningham, the "Cummy" to whom he dedicated *A Child's Garden of Verses*. In that dedication, Stevenson refers to her as "My second Mother, My first Wife," unmistakable indications of the formative influence that she had on his early years. With her help, he delighted in turning objective detail into subjective impression.

His feelings toward his parents are less obvious. As a child, he was as devoted to them as he was expected to be, fond of accompanying them on their trips to the continent and dutifully agreeable to following his father's profession. In adolescence, however, he transformed his obedience into seeming rebellion, flaunting his sham bohemianism before those who he knew would be shocked by even the slightest abnormality. His mother Margaret Stevenson, as befits the daughter of a ministerial family, was pious though not zealous; she was more troubled by her physical ailments than by mankind's sinfulness. Although she may be the model for such sickly women as Jean Weir in *Weir of Hermiston*, her ability to endure the difficult years of her son's maturity, to accompany him on his voyage to the South Seas, and indeed to outlive him testifies to her physical stamina.

Thomas Stevenson was a more complicated being. Recent study of the unpublished correspondence suggests that he was not quite the autocrat that Victorian fathers often were, yet his attempted dominance was the likely catalyst which compelled Stevenson to abandon his domestic security. (Relations between fathers and sons are traditionally among the most involved, as so many nineteenth-century novels prove.) Perhaps the best description of Thomas Stevenson appears appropriately in his son's memorial essay written shortly after his death. In "Thomas Stevenson: Civil Engineer," [3] Stevenson recalls a father whose death he can regret but never fully mourn. [4] Even as he accurately presents his father's contradictory nature, he indicates the indelible remains of their strained affection. While their differences were most severe during Stevenson's adolescence, even after his marriage and his return from America he and his father were never again so close as when Thomas dreamed of his son as another lightkeeper.

As Stevenson's poem of that name indicates, however, Thomas's son had other plans. Although he had toyed with writing awkward historical fiction as a child, he had hardly written anything more substantial than a primitive drama, which he and Henley later turned into their first collaborative venture. Yet, by 1875, Stevenson was publishing reviews, writing descriptive essays with a decided philosophical bent, and appearing as an expert in the pages of the *Encyclopaedia Britannica.* He was also appearing as a constant visitor at the artists' colony at Fontainebleu, where his cousin, Robert Mowbray Stevenson, was a regular member. Although the two were seemingly much alike, Robert Mowbray possessed an artistic flourish which his cousin could hardly emulate. While Robert Mowbray was a natural actor, Robert Louis was always aware of the realities and could but ape—ever his way—what the other would perform exquisitely. As often happens, all saw through his poor performance except his parents, who believed their son had become the vagabond that his manner suggested.

Nothing reveals Stevenson's awkwardness during this period better than his love affairs. The two that can be documented, his "potato love" for Fanny Sitwell and his marriage to the significantly older Fanny Osbourne, disclose the callow young man beneath the veneer of bohemian rascality. Fanny Sitwell was the recently separated wife of a minister—Stevenson was always attracted to at least a touch of piety—who had come to stay with one of his many cousins. There she and Stevenson met in 1873; and, while they remained friends for another twenty years, their initial association was particularly intense. Like the second Fanny of his life, Fanny Sitwell was about ten years older than Stevenson and had just freed herself from a marriage which seems to have been trying for both parties.[6] She clearly was charmed by the attentions of a younger man who was more than a bit artistically inclined. Stevenson, as well, was at the point of freeing himself from a situation he could not help but view as oppressive. Accordingly, their letters suggest their mutual needs. His contain rare moments of unguarded insecurity; hers maintain the expected restraint of her delicate position. Addressing Mrs. Sitwell with various terms of endearment, Stevenson reveals himself as he does to no one else in these years, receiving whatever comfort a respectable woman may give. She becomes his true Madonna, as he sometimes addressed her, for she is the icon in whose cold embrace he languished.

Fanny Osbourne was different. A Hoosier cosmopolite, she left home and husband in California to brave the fortunes of artistic Europe and delighted in often being the only woman in a masculine world. Already a fancied coquette in her San Francisco days, she and her grown daughter, Belle, were celebrities in the artists' colonies of Paris, Grez, and Fontainebleau. Always a vain woman beguiled by a handsome exterior, her attraction to Stevenson, after first being charmed by his cousin, may have been little more than harmless flirtation. Whatever the intention, their casual relationship soon became intimate; and by the winter of 1877 Stevenson asked his friend, Charles Baxter, to forward his mail to Fanny's Paris address.[7]

Stevenson's letters to Baxter indicate his concern over the necessary secretiveness of his affair with Fanny and his growing despair at her decision to return to America (50-56). Despite their informativeness, however, all but the surface details remain vague. Shortly after her departure, Stevenson received a telegram informing him of her illness and, with little hesitation, decided to follow after her. His trip to and across America is the substance of *The Amateur Emigrant* and *Across the Plains,* but these works omit his severe illness in Monterey and his indigent existence in San Francisco. Fanny's illness may have been a lure to bait a willing lover or it may have been less serious than she supposed. Whatever the case, their roles were soon reversed, and she became what she always thought herself to be: the physical and artistic nurse of a sickly husband—providing the necessary sustenance to insure his success.

Fanny's need to protect her husband was both helpful and harmful. In the early years of their marriage she kept him alive, but in later years she overplayed her role. Petty considerations became dominant; and, as she feared her waning influence, she attempted to assert her necessity. Although she asserted herself often, she was especially harsh toward Henley, Fanny's nemesis; for he personified that gruff, gross masculinity which she attempted to deny not only in her husband but in his friends as well. Throughout Henley's and Stevenson's years of friendship, beginning in 1875 when they first met in an Edinburgh infirmary, they maintained a closeness based upon mutual understanding though frequent disagreements occurred. Yet Fanny hardly missed an opportunity to carp at Henley, accusing him of being artistically destructive (see Chapter IV), or blaming him for her husband's illness. Stevenson was placed in the impossible position of having to choose between them, and anyone familiar with his chivalric loyalty knew exactly what that choice would inevitably be.

The precipitant occasion was seemingly a letter that Henley sent Stevenson complaining about a story that Fanny had recently published. Henley claimed that the story originally belonged to Stevenson's cousin, Katherine de Mattos, and that Fanny had in effect stolen it from her. (He was particularly incensed that Fanny did not publicly acknowledge her indebtedness.) Stevenson's reaction was characteristic although not fully comprehensible. He was certainly expected to take umbrage at Henley's accusation, but the severity of his response would have been better directed at Henley's gratuitous advice rather than at his accusation of bad faith. Since Fanny was away at the time, securing the yacht on which they were soon to sail to the South Seas, Stevenson was unable to consult her; therefore, he proceeded to reply with all the woeful agonies of a wounded knight called to defend his lady's honor at any cost. Accusation followed accusation across the Atlantic until what was once a friendship became only a memory. After the rupture with Henley, Fanny had Stevenson to herself; but she could hardly replace what Henley had been. Though she tried to be what Stevenson generously describes as "Teacher, tender comrade, wife," her lack of success produced the agonies of his final years.

Stevenson sailed to the South Seas in 1888 in pursuit of health and settled finally in Samoa because he realized that he could never again return to a climate which meant death. As his fiction hints, however, and his unedited letters prove, he failed to find the paradise he sought. Although he found temporary relief from the constant debility that he knew in Europe and America, he also found himself burdened by familial difficulties sufficient to cause the cerebral hemorrhage from which he died. Forced to depend upon his family for the companionship he had previously known among friends, he soon learned that they could not fill the need. Nor could he maintain the writing pace which they in return demanded. As Fanny's children, Lloyd and Belle, grew older, they became accustomed to the luxuries which even in the earlier years had not come easily. Not only were they unable to provide more than perfunctory service, but their wayward exploits and financial irresponsibility drained Stevenson of much needed strength. When Fanny had a nervous breakdown in 1893, he was literally on his own; and he survived another year only by the force of what was always a rather indomitable will.[8]

Stevenson's final years, like the rest of his life, were very different from the romantic picture which his idolizers constructed. Behind the gloss of the far-flung adventurer lay a dull, grim, commonplace reality whose details they attempted to hide. At first, they tried to shape his life according to their model; and, after only a partial success, they denied him any other life in death. Sidney Colvin would write him scraps of advice complaining about Stevenson's waning talent and his wasted efforts amid a savage population, urging him to return home while knowing that he would have given all but his life to do so. After his death, his friends and heirs engaged in a sordid squabble in an effort to enrich themselves by keeping his reputation artificially pure. What they created was a wax figure with none of the essential contradictions which only Henley admitted: "A deal of Ariel, just a streak of Puck,/ Much Antony, of Hamlet most of all,/ And something of the Shorter-Catechist." [9]

If Stevenson studies have been made difficult by a biography that pretends to be life, they have been equally complicated by letters that pose as complete.[10] Yet neither can be totally blamed for the vagaries of his literary reputation. Still a popular writer, though fewer titles remain identifiable with him, his popularity is often held against him as an indication that his literature is suitable only to the less sophisticated. Indeed, the most popular titles are usually found in children's editions. Confining Stevenson to the nursery, however, is to confuse his method with his audience. Few writers have captured the emotions of childhood quite so well and therefore need to be read so much by adults. Few writers, furthermore, have been so challenged by the difficulties of life beyond childhood, and few have been so reluctant to accept defeat. Stevenson's fictional world is tempered by a childlike imagination because he would not admit to the despair which logic dictated. Instead, he chose an alogical world, a fantasized reality whose grimness was less apparent though no less certain.

The romantic position, however, created unintended complications. Although Stevenson structured his narratives so that they might penetrate the deepest layers of the psyche, they were not always able to do so with the intensity he wished. Too often his intentions and his material worked against each other, and the result was tentative, suggestive but incomplete. This criticism is as applicable to his more successful works as to those that now only appear in the collected editions. His problem was both stylistic and philosophical. Stylistically, Stevenson's strength lay in the sharp effect—a telling phrase and a rousing situation; philosophically, he believed in the certainty of failure. While the style allowed him an enviable immediacy, it also permitted a facility which often borders on the superficial. The philosophy imposed an external barrier which remained esthetically limiting. Together, they produced a literature in which vivid detail often replaced narrative development.

As a romancer, Stevenson placed himself in opposition to the major literary currents of the late nineteenth century. Although influenced by many of his contemporaries, and friend to some, he is perhaps best compared to George Meredith and Henry James. While they develop the full contours of their fiction, he depends upon suggestive implication. While they write stories which use the idiom of romance to detail the intricacies of experience, he reduces experience to gesture and symbol. While they wish to reveal the complexity of individual psychology, he attempts to awaken the collective unconscious. As a master of romance, Stevenson has few equals, but he paid the price of achievement. That necessary distinction of fictional method which he upheld so vigorously in precept and practice became blurred beneath the popular clamor for greater realism. First Meredith and then James developed techniques which opened the way for narrative to become a handmaiden of psychology into what Joseph Conrad appropriately called "the heart of darkness." In comparison, Stevenson is a figure much like the old lamplighter he recalls in a celebrated essay. Not content to be a light-keeper like his father, he set out to become a light-giver, but his Promethean powers were limited. Striking the flame of an old gaslight soon to be retired, he illuminates only part of the "palpable obscure."

CHAPTER 2

No More the Melancholy Jacques

ALTHOUGH Stevenson achieved his popularity as a writer of fiction, he began his literary career as an essayist. From his first published essay "Roads" (November, 1973), to his last "My First Book: *Treasure Island*" (August, 1894), he continued to write essays with a regularity shared only by the poetry. Yet most readers today either disregard the essays entirely or treat them as Stevensonian samplers from which to cull appropriate reflections upon life and literature.[1] There is much in the essays—an elaborate and overly self-conscious style, a homiletic directness, and a posturing meant to resemble wisdom—which explains their current disfavor but which also provides their rhetorical strength and their Stevensonian identity. A balanced view of the essays, therefore, acknowledges their limitations (an unavoidable quality of Stevenson's literature) while it also recognizes an accompanying artistry (a corollary of the first).

Stevenson's essays present a measure of his artistic and personal growth, a guide to his philosophy, and an esthetic equivalent of his other writings. Thematically and structurally, they contain ideas he was to extend in his fiction: man as pilgrim on a journey to an illusive salvation; the blessings of nonachievement and the paradoxical necessity of action; the consequences of the clash between civilization and its barbaric sediment. The result in both forms is an attitude which is best described as a shrug-of-the-shoulders fatalism and an ability which is immediately compelling but ultimately disappointing.

As the "sedulous ape" he claimed to be,[2] Stevenson does not often submit to fruitful dissection. Specific essays, or parts thereof, contain elements of Sir Francis Bacon's moral earnestness, Michel Montaigne's autobiographical speculations, Charles Lamb's self-centered playfulness, and William Hazlitt's verbal and syntactic directness.[3] The influences are so numerous that they serve only as a partial introduction; therefore, the best way to approach Stevenson's essays is to approach them directly, investigating those details that make them peculiarly Stevensonian.

The nominal subject of his first essay, "Roads," is a stroll upon those mountain byways whose suggestive surroundings provide both transport and transportation. The transportation is necessarily ambulatory while the transport follows only from a consciously formal attitude, an epistemological process whose principles are drawn from the Wordsworthian cottage. The essay attempts to detail the necessary elements of that process and, in doing so, becomes more than a simple piece of topographical description. It dwells upon the physical to describe what is essentially a spiritual experience, and it forms a union of precept and practice where the experience of the walker serves as a paradigm for a way of life which is meant to be both salutary and sufficient. The little country road assumes a dimension beyond its narrow confines, and the essay extends beyond topography to typology.

Although "Roads" is a preliminary excursion, it offers noteworthy examples of Stevenson's method as an essayist. Viewing himself as a "Victorian Sage," he establishes the essay as an instrument of prophetic wisdom in which style and content are indivisible. The reader is constantly aware of an authorial hand balancing the scales of logic and sense, manipulating the suggestions of aphorism and example, joining the meaning of literal and symbolic. Stevenson opens the essay with a truism placed in a compound sentence whose intricate balance is meant to suggest the difficult action which its substance conveys, to evaluate nature as a form of art. He follows this assertion with a seeming denial and then qualifies that by admitting that artistic sensitivity is indeed necessary to natural appreciation. He concludes the paragraph by affirming that in both it is necessary to "seek out [a] small sequestered loveliness."

Having established the direction of the essay, Stevenson details the procedures necessary to meaningful appreciation. He first indicts certain popular fallacies: that the awesome contemplation of mountainous grandeur is the proper response to nature, that only the man "in city pent" can truly appreciate the countryside. Denying these, he substitutes his own guidelines in which "every gratification should be rolled long under the tongue." Combining esthetic principles with sensual pleasures, he establishes his traveler as more pilgrim than pedestrian, who is in search of a unity which only he can provide. As so often in Stevenson's essays (indeed, in all of his literature), the individual is alone amid a natural isolation whose properties are dependent on "the eye of the beholder." Nature is morally neutral, and its value comes from an attitude that is admittedly artificial but no less requisite.

Stevenson's road becomes a path to other natural pleasures and a part of nature with its own beneficent inspiration. To travel that road is to journey beyond the horizon of possibility into a void of unlimited futurity. Although the end may be unrealized, the pursuit itself is sufficient. As he concludes the essay, Stevenson illustrates the ideal: man is marching at the rear of a great army struggling through life, dreaming of his jubilant arrival within the gates of the city.

The typical elements of a Stevenson essay are already partially contained in "Roads." They form a synthesis of structure and content delineating the necessities of individual action as a measure of vital experience. This synthesis is often concretized by aphorism, anecdote, and personal reminiscence. Furthermore, it is held together by a delicate balance of paradox and antithesis which is so prevalent throughout the essays that it has been commented upon by four separate critics.[4] What these critics fail to do, however, is relate this necessary dialectic to Stevenson's predominant philosophy as it appears throughout the essays and in much of the fiction. If Stevenson's use of paradox and antithesis is indeed "unique," as Snyder asserts, then its rhetorical balance should serve to identify his style.

Stevenson frequently forms his essays around commonly accepted antitheses and then proceeds not only to diminish their rhetorical and substantive distinctions but to qualify them to such an extent that their opposition (and indeed the entire dialectic) is neutralized to the point of near insignificance. He purposely uses a highly logical procedure in order to undermine not only the procedure but also its referents. What he wishes to exemplify is that, while it is necessary to realize the potential similarity in an assumed antithesis, it is also necessary to recognize that the mirror image of any truth is not only its double but its death.

Both structure and content follow the pattern of initial tension, eventual modification, and final negation. In "Aes Triplex"

(1878), for example, a contextual scheme is predicated upon the establishment of antitheses whose ambivalences make possible their eventual denial. To oppose life and death in an initial rigidity is to open the way for flexibility, for the introduction of contradictory experience whose practical realities cannot help but broaden the absoluteness of the theoretical. Stevenson's intention is to reduce the force of the constrictively theoretical by presenting actual practice sufficient to contradict the accepted position. If contemplation of death is thought to have an unhealthy influence upon life's activities, then men should imitate those who conduct their lives with little thought of finality. Men should adopt a mental and emotional shield of triple brass, and then transcend, if only momentarily, the passive confines of an outworn tradition. Such an attitude invariably involves struggle: struggle between theory and practice, between the old and the new, between the promise and the achievement. Such a struggle is the essence of Stevenson's literature, for the individual battles the cosmic forces outside of himself and the psychic forces within.

The perplexing exhortations in "Aes Triplex" go beyond the proverbial wisdom of "Roads." Caught in a complexity of verbal and thematic forces, they offer in place of clear direction a vague possibility made less substantial in a world of inevitable striving and invariable paradox. Moreover, the attempted resolution of both the struggle and the paradox often falls short of completion. Left with no certainty of achievement, Stevenson turns inward upon the tensions contained in the essay and constructs from them a process where action and not completion is the measure of being. Undirected action, however, revolves upon itself, growing increasingly self-reflective and finally self-destructive. Method and matter produce the only possible result: a shrug-of-the-shoulders and a stiff upper lip while one waits for an indefinite end.

I Critical Essays

What was true of "Roads" and "Aes Triplex" is applicable to many of Stevenson's other essays. Whether their subject is a particular individual (in the critical essay), solitary travelers (in the topographical reminiscence), or Stevenson himself (in the travel narrative), they form a continuous illustration of his attempt to join structure and content. Stevenson's critical essays may be divided into three separate types: the book review, the subjective impression of a literary figure, and the manifesto. The reviews were written mainly between 1874 and 1876, and they are relatively slight pieces which reveal more about Stevenson than about their specific subjects. Whether in "Jules Verne's Stories," or in "On Lord Lytton's Fables in Song," Stevenson's chief interest (when not himself) is the author and his ability and willingness to express himself in his writings. His two essentials are "sincerity" and "gusto" (both reminiscent of Hazlitt), and his application of these characteristics to the several authors he chooses to consider provides a fairly accurate guide to his own literary practice.

In the essay on Lytton's fables, for example, he distinguishes between the traditional fable as presented by Aesop and La Fontaine and their modern equivalents as written by Lytton and himself: "We find ourselves in presence of quite a serious, if quite a miniature, division of creative literature . . . and the fable begins to take rank with all other forms of creative literature, as something too ambitious, in spite of its miniature dimensions, to be resolved in any succinct formula without the loss of all that is deepest and most suggestive in it" (V, 281). Stevenson's own fables are much like those he describes, for he develops them from an overtly didactic form of literature which he turns toward characteristic ambiguity. Likewise, his discussion of Jules Verne allows him to state his principles of characterization in an adventure story and to specify his subsequent practice of treating his characters like "puppets" in a medium appropriately free from psychological detail.

The longer critical essays are broader and more ambitious. Unlike the previous essays, they were collected and published in book form during Stevenson's lifetime, either in *Familiar Studies of Men and Books* (1882) or *Memories and Portraits* (1887). Written for the most part during his apprenticeship, they combine the specific focus of the review with the theoretical exposition of the manifesto. The earliest of these, "Victor Hugo's Romances" (August, 1874), is primarily a discussion of Stevenson's view of romance. Placing Hugo in relation to Henry Fielding and Sir Walter Scott, he constructs a progressive development from the rather static, one-dimensional fiction of Fielding, in which characters were composed of easily recognizable components and background was little more than tableau, to the richer fiction of Scott in which the intricate relationship between character and environment begins to be suggested if not yet fully delineated. Hugo, as a writer of romance, treats the form as an extension of the actual which forces immediate recognition of man's conflict with circumstances he must confront. For Stevenson as well, romance is the vehicle by which the private individual is made to realize his kinship with the universal forces which challenge all. The romancer brings these forces into the scheme of his narrative by treating character and background as inseparable.

As if to exemplify their necessary relation, Stevenson's essay on "John Knox and his Relations to Women" (1875) is an interesting attempt to write a nonfictional romance based on the several conflicts in Knox's life. While occasionally smug in his relish of Knox's hypocrisy, Stevenson fashions an essay which is an admirable exploration of the complexities of character and the unpredictability of resultant action. Upbraided for being unpolitic in his exhortations against women, Knox was yet able to use this directness to his advantage in his later battles with Queen Mary and Queen Elizabeth; unclear as a stylist, his ambiguous declarations drove his disciples to a beneficial pragmatism; less diplomatic than Calvin, he was still able to achieve his purpose with a success unknown to his mentor. Because of his inconsistencies Knox emerges with all the fascinating shadings of an intriguing portrait. He is shown to possess inescapable human frailties over which he triumphs—often despite himself.

The strength of the Knox essay is that it sets in relief the essential conflict between action and achievement. Stevenson's other treatments of those who withdraw from immediate action— Charles of Orleans and Henry David Thoreau—in contrast to such men of action as François Villon and Walt Whitman, develop this conflict even further. His two essay excursions into American literary figures provide a balanced view of the problem. In Whitman, "The Gospel According to Whitman," (1878), Stevenson finds a kindred spirit who is much that he would like to be, a prophet shouting his message in tones that are strident without being hollow. Whitman preaches the gospel of optimism, predicated upon freedom from social rigidity and the creation of a new, national literature opposed to the earlier poetry of despair.

His poetry prompts the reader to significant action by waking him to that which he should know: the ability to transcend the unthinking response. Whitman creates a poetry of love in which the individual is free from constraint although bound by his love for others.

Thoreau, on the other hand, is guilty of a morbid self-centeredness ("Henry David Thoreau: His Character and Opinions" [1880]). Troubled by many of the same concerns as Whitman, he can never divorce himself from their consideration. Ungenerous, content to be merely a dissenter, Thoreau is little more than a skulker from life, intent solely upon his little self-world. Unfair as this estimate may be (Stevenson admits his bias in the Preface to *Familiar Studies*), it nonetheless sharply reveals Stevenson's uncomfortableness with inaction, even if legitimately motivated. Previously, in his consideration of Charles of Orleans (1876), he had depicted a man much like Thoreau who is caught up in circumstances which he is incapable of meeting without a cloying sense of his limitations. Charles's answer is to retire from the active life into an artificial society, there to compose poetry. Although Stevenson is sympathetic to his dilemma, he nonetheless upbraids him for his cowardice and accuses both him and Thoreau of unpardonable self-indulgence.

Stevenson's partial response to what Charles and Thoreau represent may be found in "Talk and Talkers, I and II" (1882). Intended as amusing portraits of Stevenson's closest friends—Henley, Fleeming Jenkin, Sir Walter Simpson, and John Addington Symonds—they provide at the same time what might be regarded as a gentlemanly ethic. Witty, sophisticated, urbane, the essays are infused with these qualities because the behavior they illustrate is a necessary complement of right action. Social conversation becomes not merely a verbal exercise but a total activity which removes the mind from a dangerous lassitude and thrusts it into a simulation of battle. Talk forces one to engage in direct relation to another and forbids the promptings of the dissolute self to prevail. In conversation, one stands triumphant upon the fallen egotism of the recluse.

The third type of critical essay, the literary manifesto, attempts to produce esthetic wisdom in the form of the familiar essay at the same time that it promotes insight into Stevenson's method.

Of these essays, "A Gossip on Romance" (1884) is the most important. Arguing from psychology, as well as from folk tradition, Stevenson considers romance to be an elemental human ingredient representative of an instinctive response to particularly striking stimuli: brute incident as it meets the brute being. Distinguishing between drama as "poetry of conduct" and romance as "the poetry of circumstance," he theorizes that the second is necessarily amoral, dealing as it must with an individual placed amid circumstances whose challenge he must meet with an immediacy which precludes careful decision. Incident is the fictional apparatus by which submerged psychological urges are brought to the surface by a combination of events too powerful to allow concealment. Romance serves as the concretization of the unconscious. Each particular striking incident partakes of multiple associations, associations relative not only to specific places or specific people—Friday's footprint, Deacon Brodie's cabinet—but reminiscent of all human history. Each man is a creature of archetypal experience, and the purpose of romance, with its archetypal suggestions, is to elicit a significant response.

Stevenson's own response to romance was to be its champion both in theory and in practice. When he found it attacked, he rose to its defense; and both "A Note on Realism" (1883) and "A Humble Remonstrance" (1884) have as their central thesis the importance of romance amid a world of alien forces threatening its legitimacy and attempting to install themselves in its place. In the first essay, Stevenson criticizes those modern authors (notably Emile Zola) who sacrifice the "beauty and significance of the whole to local dexterity . . . and, with scientific thoroughness, steadily . . . communicate matter which is not worth learning. . . ." Viewing romance as a form which insists that significant detail be integral to the entire narrative, Stevenson regards realism as a violation of that purpose. Formerly a narrative device designed to broaden an individual's involvement with his environment, it has degenerated into the admission of detail for its own sake. Equally grievous, this greater attention to detail has been confused with veracity; and realism, instead of being rightfully considered a technical device, has gained independent authority. For Stevenson, all art is imitation; therefore, the distinction is not between truth and falsehood but between the kind of literature that an author chooses to create.

No More the Melancholy Jacques

In "A Humble Remonstrance," Stevenson reaffirms what he finds essential in the art of fiction. Literature is not in competition with life, he says, but is a selection from life—"a significant simplification" in which chaos, illogicality, and confusion are ordered into a pattern which is neat, finite, and self-contained. Literature takes its validity not from fact but fiction, not in its illustration of life but in its distillation from life. Fiction is an artistic device which permits the manipulation of actuality beyond its limited possibilities. Neither true nor false to life, it is complementary to it in a way that romance may be said to be complementary. It is therefore essential that the artistry of a work be immediately apparent as incident is telegraphic in romance, for all art is meant to call men away from their adherence to commonplace toward a realization of their potential.

II Topographical and Reminiscent

Fond of quoting the lines "out of my country and myself I go," [5] Stevenson might better have used as his motto Wordsworth's "A Traveller I am/ Whose tale is only of himself"; for this quotation aptly describes his topographical and reminiscent essays. Forced to travel in his youth because of ill health (his own and his parents'), and fond of traveling because of its modishness, Stevenson attempts to make his adult travels a philosophical experience in which he appears as both subject and object. His plan is to deal with each of the topographical essays within the broader context of a sentimental journey (somewhat in the manner of Lawrence Sterne) in which the power of his personality will both lend and receive impressions necessary to a full and meaningful appreciation and exposition.

In the short essays, the self is prominent, the direction centripetal. Wishing to escape, or at least lay down, the burden of existence, Stevenson attempts to withdraw into an arcadia, a forest of Arden straight out of his favorite Shakespearian play, where he may free himself from the call of history. Fearful of what nature itself may represent (it was not always easy to be a romantic in a Darwinian age), he insures that it will be salutary by bringing to it appropriate associations. As he says in "On The Enjoyment of Unpleasant Places" (1874), seemingly unpleasant surroundings may produce pleasant sensations in that they force the individual to exercise his will in order to reverse the negative.

If this is so, then the ease of self-discovery and self-expression in pleasant surroundings is all the more apparent. "An Autumn Effect" (1875), "A Winter's Walk in Carrick and Galloway" (written in 1876 but not published until 1896), and "Forest Notes" (1876) emphasize the natural affinity which Stevenson as a traveler achieves amidst the inspiratory atmosphere of England, Scotland, and France.

"Forest Notes" in particular, since it is also a description of the artist's colony of which he was for some years a devoted if not constant member, is a special paean to freedom, to the joys of a new society located in an atmosphere suitable to its principles. The forest is simultaneously removed from the restrictions of an oppressive history and is the incarnation of a more profound history responsive to man's basic needs. A "blessed bower" offering escape from life's exigencies, it is a paradise holding out promise of the Hesperidean golden apples in place of "the fruit/ Of that forbidden tree whose mortal taste/ Brought death into the world, and all our woe."

The remainder of the topographical essays do little more than reiterate these prescriptions. "Walking Tours" (1876), as its title implies, repeats the injunction (with echoes from William Hazlitt's "On Going On a Journey") to withdraw from the control of temporality by pursuing a journey into eternity; "Memoirs of an Islet" (1887) details the escape into an aboriginal time, a prehistory removed from life's strangulation; and "Fontainebleau" (1884), much as the earlier "Forest Notes," remembers a Stevensonian arcadia "where the young are more gladly conscious of their youth, [and] the old better contented with their age."

The reminiscent essays may be distinguished from the others by a content which is overtly didactic and by a structure which emphasizes Stevenson's homiletic intentions. Perhaps no other essays were so widely read during his lifetime, and surely few others have since been so widely disregarded. Often annoyingly self-centered, they present ethical imperatives in a wisdom-literature in which theme and structure emphasize the rhetorical manipulations so characteristic of the Stevenson essay. Concerned with childhood, love, marriage, age, youth and the general minutiae of daily conduct, they extend the aphoristic tendencies of the other essays and codify the Stevensonian moral.

The most typical are collected under the title of the earliest, *Virginibus Puerisque* (1881). Sounding at times like the topographical essays in their emphasis upon solitude, they also recognize the complementary and somewhat contradictory need for companionship. Himself much in need of friends,[6] Stevenson plays upon the disparity between intellectual isolation and physical necessity. Like a minor Carlyle, he draws love out of the laws of causality and views it as analogous to mystical revelation, a transitory, not everlasting, yea in the history of everyman. Unlike Carlyle's Teufelsdrockh, Stevenson's everyman is not able to conduct his life within a pattern that leads eventually to salvation. Stevenson's love is a physical union, a joining which, if vital, is nonetheless mortal. In his world, there is neither Christian afterlife nor Platonic transcendence: people live, love, and die with little more than a galvanic twitch of the muscle.

Stuck with his cynicism, Stevenson attempts to find some consolation in idleness, but his insistence on its enforced maintenence only emphasizes its limitations. Initially a corollary of solitude, and thus a direct response to the doctrine of utility, it soon becomes self-indulgence and mere posturing. His parody of John Bunyan in "An Apology for Idlers" illustrates his predicament. A dialogue between an Idler and Mr. Worldly Wiseman, meant to appear as an echo of "Expostulation and Reply" with an anti-Christian bias, reveals instead the shallowness of the idler's position. Christian's road into experience becomes a lonely grotto and his journey to the New Jerusalem becomes a retreat from the responsibilities of the old.

Escape, like all else in Stevenson, is temporary. The human condition is to be trapped in an endless struggle and, do what one will, the forces of that conflict are always present. In fact, Stevenson is so taken by their presence that he includes them even in such a piece of nostalgia as "A Plea for Gas Lamps" (1878). Often thought to be little more than a sentimental glance backward, this essay is instead a muted example of man's constant battle with literal and metaphoric darkness. Openly compared to Prometheus, the lamplighter offers an antiquated attempt to cope with the "universal darkness [which] belies all." Caught between an underlying barbarism and a veneer of civilization, man is compelled to struggle for survival, to endure "the war in the members." As Stevenson suggests in another essay, "A Penny

Plain and Twopence Coloured," he must see the world colored with possibilities even though he knows that what he sees before him may be only a cardboard reality.

III *The Travel Narratives*

Considered as extended essays, the travel narratives turn precept into example by thrusting the philosophical self of the shorter essays into the foreground as Stevenson the traveler who personally proceeds on a voyage "outward bound." Considered as semifiction, autobiographical fact modified by the demands of artistic manipulation, they represent a purposely ordered journey whose initial impulse is linear but whose final direction is circular —an outward movement wherein the physical journey beyond the "golden gate" becomes a spiritual journey to recapture "the voice of generations dead." In search of physical health and spiritual solace, Stevenson found the first possible only at the agonizing cost of permanent exile; and he sought the second in memories of his homeland only after painfully realizing that the New World to which he sailed was actually a brute replica of the Old World. The travel narratives, therefore, like the shorter essays, result in ultimate futility. They are the practical correlatives of the homiletic exhortation to act despite inevitable failure.

An Inland Voyage (1878) describes a canoe trip down the Oise River in the company of Sir Walter Simpson, a trip filled with all the playfulness of assumed names (the Cigarette and the Arethusa), mistaken identity (they are thought to be peddlers), and occasional misadventure (an overturned boat). Though filled with much humor, the trip is more than a pleasant journey through the continent. Stevenson's quotation from Andrew Marvell's "Bermudas" (a song of Protestant martyrs fleeing from persecution) points to a seriousness which his preface reinforces. There he indicates that the purpose of *An Inland Voyage* is to serve as a record of positive relation between man and nature, a journey into the wilderness in which initial flight results in a celebration of God's universe. The conclusion, however, suggests that the celebration may be possible only upon return, for "the most beautiful adventures are not those we go to seek."

An Inland Voyage, moreover, is a journey not only into nature but into the self. As the literal journey is an attempt to withdraw from a restrictive society, the metaphorical journey is an acknowledgment that self-freedom is as much an attitude as an action, especially since that action is doomed to failure. A major ingredient of this attitude is humor, the playfulness of the condemned steeled to endure hardship while glorying in possibilities that obscure the inevitable end. The humor of *An Inland Voyage,* like so much in Stevenson, has a double role: while it entertains, it never allows the reader to forget the grim reality which inspires it.

The humor of *Travels With a Donkey* (1879) is equally engaging but likewise somewhat transparent. Any account of travels through a foreign country with a bulky, balky beast of burden is likely to be amusing. Yet when the beast of burden turns out to be oneself, the amusement is less than uproarious; and the intended lesson is driven home with an inversion that goes straight to the center of Stevenson's philosophy. In his dedication to Sidney Colvin, Stevenson immediately sets the symbolic frame: "we are all travellers in what John Bunyan calls the wilderness of this world—all, too, travellers with a donkey; and the best that we find in our travels is an honest friend" (I, 149). Setting forth upon this wilderness like a Diogenes in search of both truth and friendship, Stevenson meets several people from peasants to monks, but he finds little honesty and no friend. Forced to rely upon an innocent but stubborn animal whom, in Coleridge fashion, he is reluctant to brutalize, he finally bears the physical burden himself, thereby creating an inversion which is both a reversal of proper roles and a comic analogue of Christian's journey. As Stevenson proceeds on his journey, he recognizes the comedy of his situation. Wishing freedom, he finds himself instead joined to a donkey who refuses to perform her expected duties; wishing to travel for travel's sake, to move beyond "the feather-bed of civilization," he finds that he must purchase his freedom from the burdens of travel only to return to those of an existence he once hoped to abandon.

Although some laughter remains in the later travel narratives, it is tempered by the vivid details of Stevenson's broadened experience. In *The Amateur Emigrant* (1879), he is no longer able to travel with all the trappings of luxury. He now finds himself one step above steerage and learns for the first time the anguish of those who have to travel out of their country (though not out of themselves). Not always sympathetic to his fellow passengers,

[33]

he begins to comprehend their poverty and their enforced exile; and travel is no longer a metaphysical exercise but a pitiful condition. As Stevenson confronts the hungry and the oppressed, the casual traveler of the early essays becomes a fellow traveler on a journey marked by grim reality.

As his travels proceed from ship to train, from the Clyde to the Pacific, realistic details become the rule. The nauseating railroad cars of the emigrant train, the itch which plagues him throughout his trip across the plains, and the mixed relief and uncertainty with which he first sights a resplendent San Francisco combine to signify a willingness to deal with experience that is absent from his earlier writings. Artistic embellishment takes second place to vivid and often grossly forthright description; philosophy and rhetoric, to situations not easily structured.

Stevenson's next travel book, *The Silverado Squatters* (1883), is a record of the strange honeymoon that he, Fanny, and Lloyd spent in an abandoned silver mine on Mt. Saint Helena in California's Napa Valley. Although he attempts to invest the California countryside with many of the romantic associations characteristic of the Edenic landscape he attempted to find in Europe, the title contradicts any hoped-for permanence. Only a squatter in a rank and unweeded garden, Stevenson is unable to avoid the difficulties he found before. Characteristically, he faces these with much charm, a playfulness which masks some of the underlying hardship, and a fortitude which increases as the difficulties mount. Nonetheless, his mountain refuge is at best an ambiguous Juan Silverado, replete with all of the complexities of the fictional character who shares its name.

Stevenson's final journey to the South Seas, exemplifies all the romantic adventure which his readers expected of him yet it also epitomizes his failure to put any part of his life behind him. Traveling for the first time out of the known Western world, hoping to escape "the shadow of the Roman empire," he learns that neither in his life nor in his literature is he able to "lie down with the Ten Commandments." Instead, as he travels farther into the tropics he is constantly thrown back upon reminders of his native land, to comparisons between Highlanders and Islanders, to a recognition that "so simply, even in South Sea Islands, and so sadly, the changes come."

No More the Melancholy Jacques

In the unfinished letters entitled *In The South Seas*,[7] Stevenson attempts to communicate some of his impressions of that journey to "the fireside traveller." Embarking on a voyage prompted by failing health, he structures the letters as if they were an account of adventurous travel beyond civilization, a reversal of Tennyson's embracement of Western society. At the outset, he sails away from a world grown moribund to an island culture whose innocence and purity represent the very qualities which Victorian society has all but destroyed. Establishing himself as a modern Ulysses, Stevenson turns his back upon an outworn Ithaca and sails forward "to seek a newer world."[8]

In the South Seas, however, he confronts numerous examples of native barbarism, indolence, superstition, and depravity. While he attempts to excuse much of what he sees by comparison with an equally deficient Europe, and although he blames the white man for native corruption, he cannot hide his ultimate disappointment. His tropical paradise is a reminder of what civilization has barely concealed. Rather than the other side of an outworn society, it is the underside, the subliminal reality of a stylized masquerade. Left with only a barely satisfying nostalgia, he clings to a memory that becomes the center of his life and his fiction. The journey that began as a search for the forest of Arden becomes a lament for a lost identity: "Home no more home to me, whither must I wander?"[9]

CHAPTER 3

A Skelt-Drunken Boy

THAT Stevenson wrote plays is a surprise even to those who have some knowledge of his literature. Surely he would have preferred it so. Of all his lesser known works, he had least confidence in his plays, although he devoted time and energy to their creation, shared in the wavering enthusiasm which they produced, and at one time hoped they would provide an income sufficient to free him from the constant pressure of writing.[1] His ambivalence suggests that, despite the plays' financial and literary failure, his experience as playwright and as collaborator was more meaningful than has been thought. Ironically, as he became less confident of their money-making potential, he became increasingly certain of the kind of drama he wanted to write while simultaneously aware of his inability to create such drama. Coupled with this increasing self-frustration were the often-divergent views of Henley with whom he wrote four plays. There is little doubt that a chief reason for the plays' lack of success was that too often he and Henley were operating under conflicting dramatic theories.

Few would argue that, had Stevenson pursued the drama more vigorously, or had he worked alone, his plays would have emerged with more quality than they now possess. Indeed, they all make uniformly poor reading (with the possible exception of *Macaire*), and their abortive theatrical career has proved them not much better on the stage. To dismiss the plays, however, as thoroughly ephemeral (Furnas) or to designate them as Henleyian devices calculated to entrap a naive Stevenson (Fanny) is both unfair and dishonest.[2] Stevenson and Henley knew what they intended in their dramatic collaboration. They failed not because they were less than sufficiently serious (Pinero), not because Stevenson imperfectly understood the requirements of dramatic action (Swinnerton), but because they were two highly conscientious literary men who attempted to bring to the drama qualities which each believed necessary but which both were powerless to produce.[3]

I *The Collaboration*

When Stevenson and Henley began their collaboration in 1878, their first venture was an attempted resurrection of an old boyhood play of Stevenson's based on the legendary life of the noted Edinburgh criminal, Deacon Brodie. Both were impressed by French drama and melodrama,[4] and they fashioned the play for Henry Irving who had recently come to prominence at the Lyceum as the actor-manager of lavishly equipped productions of marked French provenance. But from the very beginning their contribution was uneven. Whatever Stevenson knew about French drama, he had little knowledge of the London theater (he was in the Cevennes when the project began); but Henley was already editor and dramatic critic of *London*. Stevenson's knowledge of drama came not from actual stage production, although he did act at some amateur theatricals at the Fleeming Jenkins', but from the cardboard re-creations of popular melodrama that he had marveled at as a child.[5] What the collaborators did share—and it was not the strongest of ties—was a mutual enthusiasm and a need to make money, preferably as soon as possible, since Henley had recently married and since Stevenson was wavering before the same responsibility. Stevenson contributed a not-too-well-made play by which they hoped to capture the London public and insure their financial stability; Henley offered a calling card to backstage, a foothold in the greenroom, and above all encouragement.

As their work on *Deacon Brodie* progressed, and as they became separated by an ocean, their intentions toward the play (and toward drama in general) grew predictably further apart. An early joint letter to Colvin, who was both agent and literary advisor, suggests that their attitude toward the drama was originally much in line with the conventional theories of melodramatic writing and acting: "Remember, a play is emotion as a statue is marble. Incident, story, these are but the pedestal." [6] Such drama clearly results in a vehicle of the grand style wherein effect is the rationale and exaggeration the method. Subsequent letters, however, reveal that, while Henley more or less remained within this conventional view, Stevenson attempted to break away from its confines to create a drama which England was not to see until George Bernard Shaw.

The reasons for Stevenson's changing attitude are many. Between the initial writing of *Deacon Brodie* and its first London performance in 1884, he had been to America and back, battled illness and penury almost to the point of death, acquired a family and particularly a wife who was never fond of Henley yet strongly opinionated about literary and personal matters, established something of a literary reputation, and begun to interest himself more in a literature that could be both structurally engaging and psychologically valid. Clearly, each of these factors placed a strain on the collaboration. In addition, the financial failure of the *Deacon* was growing increasingly apparent; and Stevenson knew that to make it a successful play took more than simple patchwork. Several of his letters to Henley during these years call for a break from the restrictive confines of the old model, a reworking with a minimum of melodramatic effects, and a resultant drama that would be a true representation of that romantic tragicomedy which Stevenson came to believe was the essence of drama.[7]

Perhaps the most poignant of these letters, certainly the most revealing, is that of May, 1884, only part of which was published in Colvin's collection. Written from the recuperative isolation of Hyères prior to their collaboration on the final three plays (written at Bournemouth during late 1884 and 1885), the letter clarifies Stevenson's growing irritation with the restrictions which he felt the drama, as they were writing it, imposed upon him. In the published part of the letter he states not only his esthetic position but his view of life. It is, he says, essentially the romantically comic in which tragedy and comedy come together in a synthesis whose harmony is strengthened by an all-inclusive breadth. Not tragedy which is often sham heroism, but tragicomedy, a recognition of the beauty and terror of life, is what he wishes to write.

By 1884, and no doubt before then, Stevenson realized that he and Henley were pulling in opposite and opposing dramatic and personal directions and that this polarity was occasioned as much by their philosophical positions as by a particular view of the theater. Paradoxically, the "Skelt-drunken boy," who had little acquaintance with the theater, had begun to break away from a conventional rigidity which the knowledgeable dramatic critic found it impossible to transcend. Stevenson's awareness of a new drama—it is appropriate that he admired Henry Arthur Jones—was analogous to his realization of a new kind of literature: a literature which attempted to encompass all of life's contrarities in an expression which emphasized the necessity of acceptance this side of despair. Such a literature was not possible in the collaborators' present approach to the drama, although Stevenson tried to create exactly this kind of a drama in the remaining three plays and in the revised *Deacon Brodie*.

For him, the models they were using contained too much "string," conventional trappings dictated by outworn fashion rather than by the requirements of "moved representation." Dramatic fashion was caught in a cleverly contrived but ultimately meaningless procedure which devoted itself to the mechanical repetition of devices calculated to please the most primitive and shallow tastes of its audience.[8] Stevenson called for a new freedom whose roots were in the solid earth cultivated by Shakespeare and Aristophanes, a drama not conventional but dimensional, "touched with sex and laughter; beauty with God's earth for the background."

In the unpublished conclusion to his letter Stevenson applies his stated dramatic ideals directly to his present collaboration. Prompted by Fanny, he distinguishes between the tragedy which Henley sees in life and his own pursuit of "the eldorado of romantic comedy." The distinction is indicative of their growing divergence. Stevenson views tragedy and melodrama as one-dimensional, narrow expressions limited to an artistic structure whose mechanism follows its originally conceived direction with relentless and irreversible energy. But romantic comedy, that "bird-haunted" evocation of life's fluctuations, contains the elements of both laughter and tears which transcend the rigidity of inescapable logic, both artistic and experiential. Such a drama sets out to reveal life's essentials, to imitate the circumstantial vagaries which cause delight and defeat, insuring that, if "we are merely the stars' tennis balls," we can at least enjoy the game. In order to create this kind of play, Stevenson realized that the confines of the French melodrama could no longer hold them. He and Henley now needed to break away with a liberty derived from the coarse, revelatory laughter of an Aristophanes and the delicate yet earthy humor of a Shakespeare. Only then could they pursue a collaboration which would be truly complementary, and only then could they create a drama which would present both man and his world without falsification or denial.

In each of his plays, Stevenson was forced to reproduce his dramatic principles in vehicles not suitable to their presentation. His method was to use the outward structure, "the scaffolding" as he called it, to introduce characters and values foreign to its limited form. In this way he unknowingly anticipated a procedure Shaw later proved so dramatically successful. Stevenson more than Shaw, however, took undue comfort in the neutrality which tragicomedy provided. Desirous of uncovering the essentials, he had no wish to emulate Zola; he wished, instead, to pursue nightingales, and he knew that he could not do so in a forest of cardboard scenery and wooden inhabitants. Certainly after the final three plays were rather hastily written, he also knew that he could never do so with Henley.[9] Instead of a new venture, the years of dramatic collaboration marked the deteriorating relations between two friends whose meeting in an Edinburgh infirmary Stevenson had once described as "a golden dream" (unpublished letter, December, 1882). The dream was not yet shattered by 1884 (that was to come with the first of the "quarrel letters" four years later), but the plays represent an anxious pause before the impending nightmare.[10]

II The Plays

Were it not for the information provided by several unpublished letters, it would be difficult to realize the pressures under which Stevenson and Henley labored. Although their correspondence often compensated for physical separation, it did little to avert their growing artistic and personal disparity. The letters make it possible to see the effects of this disparity upon the plays. While previously it was necessary to speak of the plays as if they were the work of two men fused into a corporate whole, or to distinguish the separable parts by virtue of their quality or their resemblance to other work, it is now necessary to read the plays as the joint expression of antagonistic dramatic views. Their failure, therefore, is no more attributable to one author than to the other; indeed, that anything approaching literature emerged from this collaboration held together by a crumbling friendship is remarkable.[11]

The plays resemble each other in several ways. All melodramas of one sort or another—even *Beau Austin* is a comedy of manners spoiled by melodramatic devices—they offer successive views of similar problems, ones not always resolved by repetition. In addition, the plays offer useful insight into what has often been considered the old and the new drama: *Deacon Brodie* (at least in its first version) is much like *Paul Clifford* and *Jack Sheppard*, while *Macaire* bears favorable resemblance to Oscar Wilde's *The Importance of Being Earnest* (1895).[12]

If *Deacon Brodie* is the prototype of Stevenson's *Dr. Jekyll and Mr. Hyde* (1886), as many critics claim, it is the bare skeleton of that highly suggestive allegory. Certain motifs clearly overlap: the double life predicated upon a catastrophic misjudgment of moral values, the cowardly resort to disguise in the face of supposed societal disapproval, the calculated reversal of ethical norms in order to justify a debased existence. William Brodie, however, has neither the depth nor the integrity of Henry Jekyll, and his parochial misdeeds seem amateurish in contrast to Jekyll's metaphysical challenge. A comparison far more revealing is that between the two versions of *Brodie* and *Macaire*. Both plays are melodramas with a difference: they are distinctive for the strikingly individual rascality of their title characters. That both are philosophical rogues with a sentimental bias alone places them at variance with their predecessors; that both are caught in a circumstantial dilemma which they cannot overcome makes them suitable Stevenson "heroes" whose heroism is measured by the strength with which they accept defeat.

The major difference between the first and revised versions of *Deacon Brodie* may be measured in the successive lessening of the Deacon's villainy. In the play's first version,[13] he is acutely conscious of his diminishing superiority, proud of his criminal abilities, abusive to those who would share his agony, and he ends his foul life by attempting to implicate all of society in his nefarious actions. Yet he is not the demon that so many of his actions suggest. Though muted, and often tempered by his dominant villainy, his relations with his family and his mistress modify (and to a minor extent explain) the compulsions of his criminal behavior. The alternations are confusing and ultimately damaging to the play's effectiveness, but the suggestions of moral complexity are significant. Evidently neither Stevenson nor Henley wanted a character that was all bad, though they wanted that badness to be paramount.[14] Scenes with his old and dying father, a visit to his mistress replete with doting children, and his reformative aspirations do much to suggest the side of Brodie not often apparent. It is clear, however, that both authors were better able to suggest the villainy than the attendant circumstances: Brodie as ranter against his sister's virtue overcomes Brodie as sometime father.

Brodie revised is more intriguing although less vital than his initial incarnation. Many of the more sentimental suggestions are strengthened, but the cruder aspects of his villainy are either lessened or completely discarded. Still a father, he is now the sire of only a single infant rather than of a brood of potential disciples; still a son and brother, he is now genuinely officious in his treatment of both father and sister and cares particularly for the latter's welfare. His rascality, therefore, is necessarily modified. Where before he was conscious of his declining power, he is now plagued by his unavoidable immersion in practices which permit no release. This later change is perhaps the most significant. Although his leadership in both versions is challenged by other members of his gang, only in the second version does he see the challenge and his eventual submission as retribution for his past actions. What was originally a matter of pride becomes finally a matter of conscience.

As Stevenson's letters suggest, he was mainly responsible for the intricacies of Brodie's conscience. His suggestions as well as Henley's complaints point directly to those softening alterations which characterize the revised and subsequently published version.[15] Both he and Henley attempted to portray in the earlier Deacon a shallow rebel whose rebelliousness, though manifested in thoroughly selfish practices, is somewhat justified by society's transparent hypocrisy. Brodie is more than a little correct when he sees his own disguise as merely a parallel of the cover under which even the most respectable hide their indiscretions. His belief that all are rogues is, however, more self-justification than valid social criticism. Always on the edge of self-awareness, he chooses instead to blame others for his downfall; and he thus loses whatever potential he may have had as an exposer of social vice. Had Stevenson and Henley been willing to allow him the critical role that they at least half intended him to have, they would have had to allow him the latitude of Falstaff or the incisiveness of Macheath. Instead, they offered a Brodie of the grand gesture who is superficially active but essentially infirm.

Brodie's activism in the earlier play is conditioned by a prideful drive to retain command. If he is meant to be a noble rebel, his nobility is diminished by his inability to distinguish between pride and principle. The Brodie of the revised version, on the other hand, is too introspective to be willfully assertive. No longer rebellious, a creature of sneering mockery and sardonic defiance, he is now more concerned with self-redemption than self-aggrandizement. The second coming of Brodie presents a man more like Christ than Satan, or perhaps most like that combination of Hamlet and Antony which Henley thought so well described Stevenson. Like many of Stevenson's characters, his behavioral pattern is fixed with his first forays into crime, and he is finally a prisoner in a dungeon of his own construction. He is also a fuller character, not only because he has greater depth but because he has greater self-awareness. Yet, in typical Stevenson fashion, his newly acquired self-knowledge does not permit him release but only the ability to know why he is condemned to a hateful continuity. Artistic realization is clearly apart from existential fulfillment. Just as the first Brodie is killed trying to escape, his dying words echoing the defiance with which he has lived, so the second Brodie runs out his life upon a sword, his dying words enforcing the bitter irony that a new life can be found only in death.

Macaire, which resembles *Deacon Brodie* in surface qualities, is not only a superior play but the best of the Stevenson-Henley collaboration. Like Brodie, Macaire is a criminal who must resort to disguise in order to conceal his identity, and the play to which he gives his name is likewise based upon an older model. *Macaire's* source is the French play *Auberges des Adrèts,* made famous by Frédéric Lemaître and brought into English melodrama in 1834. Without question, Stevenson's and Henley's *Macaire* is superior to its earlier versions as well as to their other plays because its authors found both the character and dramatic form with which to express all they had gropingly tried to achieve previously.

Macaire is described as a "melodramatic farce," and such a hybrid form might seem to be beyond the powers of two fledgling playwrights. The result, however, is a fine piece of comic writing, for the blending of two dramatic forms expresses succinctly the intended comic pessimism. If melodrama is defined as an elemental dramatic form whose essence is dream and whose impulse is escape, farce may be seen as its primitive complement—as an evocation of violence to underscore man's futile attempts at transcendence.[16] Melodrama is thus much like romance as Stevenson defined it, "the poetry of circumstance" in which man's capabilities are challenged by situations in which he must react instinctively. Farce, in turn, jeeringly compounds insurmountable circumstance with malicious glee. Placed together, they form a synthesis whose strength derives from the fixed balance of its components: a story whose primary action is escape, a clever rogue whose essential impulse is artful deceit, and a series of incidents calculated to trip up the would-be manipulator. Add sophisticated and witty dialogue, sufficient sight gags and fast pacing to insure amusing action, and the right amount of intrigue, and what results is a highly comic drama whose humor, though uproarious, becomes increasingly grim the more it is seen as a futile but necessary response.

The plot of *Macaire* is appropriately simple. Macaire and his accomplice, Bertrand, stop at an inn as they make their way toward the border and freedom. The innkeeper's putative son is about to be married, and they pause to join the celebration. When the bride's father learns, however, that his future son-in-law is a foundling, he stops the marriage. During the frenzied action following this revelation, Macaire discovers that the father is actually a wealthy Marquis; and he plots to pose as the long-lost sire and thus gain some gold. Successful only briefly, his discovery occurs when the real Marquis appears and forces Macaire to attempt murder. Defeated at every turn, he is caught attempting to kill the Marquis and shot down by the local police as he tries to escape.

A comparison of plot and character between this *Macaire* and its previous versions indicates that at the time of its writing Stevenson and Henley had learned much about their craft. What

A Skelt-Drunken Boy

Stevenson had learned, as a letter written in the early stages of the play's composition makes clear, is how to work with given material and still order it to his purpose. The Macaire of his version, though no less a brigand than his earlier, more Gallic, counterparts, possesses just the right amount of contempt and perception necessary to guarantee that his social barbs will emerge with much of the sting that Brodie's lacked.

Macaire, nonetheless, remains a self-indulgent cynic whose thrusts are blunted by his constant retreat into egotism.[17] He is not, however, a sensualist: this is Bertrand's role, and their contrast emphasizes Macaire's complex balance of greed and idealism. Wishing to "leap through history like a paper hoop, and come out among posterity heroic and immortal," his masquerade may be seen as a fit metaphor for the universal human attempt to withstand life's buffets with at least the mask of nobility. Macaire's system is to view life as a game, and he succeeds until he is forced to recognize that the rules he would play by are not his to control. Brodie is a rebel against narrow social institutions; Macaire, a spokesman for human ideals. Their difference is the measure of Stevenson's dramatic maturity as the slinking thief of the Edinburgh closes becomes the cosmopolitan wayfarer in search of freedom.

Nothing better exemplifies Macaire's stature, as well as his limitations, as the empty rhetoric of his catechisms. Intended as comic inversions of Christian guides to faith, they are instead excerpts from a cynic's manual that underscore the futility of idealism but offer nothing in its place but "words, words, words." Macaire may question the materialism that he pretends to follow, but he possesses neither the ability nor the means to transcend its often bitter truths. Like the two Brodies, the unwilling continuity of Macaire's existence prevails until death; but at his death there is neither defiance nor expectation, only the metaphysical questioning with which he has attempted to challenge an unyielding universe.

Admiral Guinea is closer to its melodramatic origins than either *Deacon Brodie* or *Macaire*. Although it contains some variations upon well-worn themes, it is far too close to such nautical melodramas as Douglas Jerrold's *Black-Ey'd Susan* to allow sufficient latitude. Its machinery is pure Skelt. The nautical language, the languishing sweethearts, the shiftless sailor who wants only a chance to make good: all might just as well have been put together with pasteboard and pigment. Even the resurrection of Pew, the evil blind man of *Treasure Island,* serves only to enhance the conventional effects without adding anything to the substance. Clearly, whatever merits the play possesses depend upon its title character.

Like the John Newton upon whom he is partially modeled,[18] John Gaunt has earned the name "Admiral Guinea" by serving as a slave captain prior to his conversion to piety. In that conversion, he has attempted to erase the more unsavory reminders of his past. All that remains of his seafaring days is the old treasure chest which he uses to store mementos of his dead wife. A man who equates piety with rigidity, he must be forced to see the narrowness of his position; he must be confronted with sufficient reminders of his past actions to make him realize that Christianity is correctly measured by the breadth of human benevolence. The agents of Guinea's realization are Kit, the sailor-lover of his daughter, Aretheusa, and Pew, whose evil influence can be rejected only by an affirmation of the admiral's own moral "blindness."

The metaphor of blindness is the central image; and it serves not only to tie the play together, if somewhat clumsily, but allows it its one outstanding scene. Pew's literal blindness and Guinea's spiritual blindness are dramatically equated when Guinea is afflicted with recurrent seizures of sleepwalking in which he is as physically sightless as his nemesis. Their encounter in the play's final sequence reinforces their relationship and permits Guinea to "awaken" to a new vision of his former identity. On a darkened stage (the audience's sight is likewise dimmed), the blind Pew stumbles on a somnambulant Guinea; and their mutual groping symbolizes the inevitable misdirection of all limited vision. As Pew falls, Guinea necessarily recognizes that he was "blinded by self-righteousness" and admonishes Kit (and the audience) henceforth to walk humbly.

Despite the power of the blindness metaphor, the symbolic tissue is not strong enough to make *Admiral Guinea* an effective play; and the Admiral is not a strong enough character to compensate for its many deficiencies. What the play offers, then, is a partial study of a type of personality which always intrigued

A Skelt-Drunken Boy

Stevenson: the guilty man who would deny his past actions but nonetheless must act upon their reemergence. His narrative counterparts are Markheim, Jekyll, and particularly Gordon Darnaway, while his judgelike pretensions ally him with Attwater and Justice Weir.

In *Beau Austin*, Stevenson's and Henley's limitations remain. While the play is turned differently than the others, its internal tensions are predicated on a similar antagonism between moral society and personal responsibility. Society here is not so much civilization but rather a group of particular people whose actions constitute a charade of civilized life. Appropriate to this kind of society, Stevenson and Henley devise a comedy of manners calculated to explore the distinction between surface posture and underlying impulse. Set amid the glitter of Regency splendor, the play describes a day at Tunbridge Wells, from the opening accusation to the final acknowledgment, from defiant challenge to loving acceptance.

The play's dichotomy is that between natural and unnatural as measured by human behavior. In none of the other plays does Stevenson's vision of a bird-haunted landscape figure so prominently; in none of the other plays is that vision more dream than reality. Dorothy Musgrave, the wronged heroine, is an innocent creature from a clearly symbolic Edenside violated by a corrupted world in which she loses both her innocence and her virginity to Beau Austin, a notorious, aging rake who personifies the values of his decaying, emasculated society. Dorothy, the fallen Diana, has her devotee in Fenwick, her lover and would-be protector. When he learns of Dorothy's seduction, he reminds Beau Austin of his duty and convinces him that his reputation can be saved only if he honors Dorothy in marriage. Although the usual complications ensue, Beau Austin finally reveals his guilt before a stunned royal entourage while a tearful Dorothy gratefully accepts his name.

In a prologue written for the 1890 production, Henley calls specific attention to the underlying sexual matter which is integral to the play's meaning. Sexual battle manifested in verbal wit is basic to the kind of comedy its authors meant *Beau Austin* to be, but what is cleverly ambiguous in Wycherly's *The Country Wife* and bitingly witty in Congreve's *The Way of the World* here

[47]

gives way to the maudlin emotions of betrayal and guilt. Despite some nicely turned phrases, too much of the play's language mirrors its impotent actors and actions. Written as an exploration of "that ancient strife/ Which is the very central fact of life," the play reduces that style to a tableau of elegantly adorned actions whose surface niceties do little to mask its essential emptiness. Although a seducer, George Austin's masculinity is more gesture than gender; and his appeal is more to the decaying monuments of an ancient order than to the vigorous youth of an eternal Eden. He is a fossil; and his marriage to Dorothy, despite his "mea culpa," restores neither her nor himself to a stature worth preserving. Rather than a celebration of bygone elegance, *Beau Austin* is a caricature of Georgian days distorted by Victorian cynicism.

The mixed reactions which the play received were touched upon by George Meredith in his letter to Stevenson thanking both authors for dedicating *Beau Austin* to him.[19] What Meredith objected to most, despite his general approval of the play, was the insistence on Dorothy's seduction. He argued that it would have been better had she been only compromised, for this would remove the stain to her reputation and also lessen significantly the vulgarity which severely dominates her motivation and her actions. Although both authors rejected this advice, Meredith was presenting a correctly Meredithian point of view. As a supreme stylist in the comedy of manners, he rightly perceived that their difficulties increased as they adhered to a dramatic form which limited rather than complemented their thematic intentions. Stevenson and Henley had a play in mind much like Jones's *The Masqueraders* or the less effective Reade-Taylor *Masks and Faces*, yet seemingly they could never fully make up their minds as to whether they wished to strip society bare or glorify its protective finery. Intending to revive an essential Pan, they instead draped an inconsequential Beau.

III *The End*

While in the throes of *Deacon Brodie*, Henley wrote to Stevenson of the ugly and its necessary recognition: "It is vain to *escamoter* the ugly. It's an essential in modern art; it is to us, perhaps, what the Beautiful was to the Greeks." [20] None of Henley's other letters on the drama so well summarizes his artistic attitude or so clearly indicates his distance from his collaborator. With prophetic insight into modern literature, Henley recognized what Stevenson was unwilling to admit. Often displeased at the "part of me that broods on the evil in the world and man," [21] Stevenson wished to create a literature which would acknowledge evil's presence without allowing its dominance. In the four plays with Henley he tried to achieve a drama that would maintain the balance he felt was necessary to successful art, but the form and his collaborator worked against him. Fond of striking incident, intimate style, broad symbolic patterns, he was at odds with the requirements of a dramatic structure which theoretically he knew well but which practically he could not manage. Fortunately, he recovered quickly from the plays' failure; but he never recovered from the failure of his collaboration with Henley. What began in the exuberance of promised success dissolved into the grim reality (inevitably petty) of an untempered accusation.

CHAPTER 4

Runes Among the Heather

STEVENSON'S poems, like his plays, are usually placed among the lower orders of his creation. His own estimate of his limited poetic ability is often accepted as an accurate, if somewhat exaggerated, admission: "A kind of prose Herrick, divested of the gift of verse, and you behold the Bard. But I like it" (Letters, II, 132).[1] Yet while his crudities are always emphasized, his personal satisfaction is often omitted.[2] Stevenson, who well knew that his medium was prose, never attempted to deny the prosaic quality of his verse; but he attempted to indicate that as occasional poems which allowed him to capture a mood or express a sentiment they had value beyond esthetic consideration. At times, he was able to create poems which transcend the personal, although most of his poems merit their present neglect. Inferior as a poet to whomever he chose to imitate,[3] he was yet able to write a series of poems about his childhood which has become a classic of children's literature; and other poems in his native Scots which are acknowledged as a major influence on the modern "makars."[4] His poems are therefore best considered as he would have them considered—as minor but intriguing attempts by a prose stylist to broaden the reaches of his art.

I Occasional Poems in English

Spanning the years of his artistic production, Stevenson's occasional poems in English deal with such diverse yet complementary topics as love, sex, perseverance, travel, and death. Many were personally chosen by him for inclusion in his collected volumes of poems, but others had to await publication until after his death.[5] Of those omitted from the collected editions, an early group, which dates from 1869–1879, serves as verse equivalents of the agonized letters he wrote to Mrs. Sitwell and to Charles Baxter during these years. With a strange yet characteristic combination of candor and affectation, Stevenson writes about the frustrations of physical desire and his concomitant wish for an easeful death amid the comforting embrace of a fallen woman. A poem of 1871 (Smith, 60) details his youthful reaction after reading *Antony and Cleopatra*. Driven by "a hunger of hopeless things," pursued by "objectless desire," he longs to expire in Cleopatra's arms rather than be alive amid such sexual torment. Another of approximately the same date (Smith, 83) accuses nature of being a Satanic conspirator bent upon his fleshly temptation (an interesting combination of Marvell and Wordsworth), and he details his longing for some "opiate for desire," preferably among the favors of "an amber lady/ Who has her abode/ At the lips of the street/ In prisons of coloured glass."

In these poems, Stevenson is not only obviously imitative but grossly self-conscious. In some, he sounds like a Whitman *manqué*, forcing an alliance with the hunchback and prostitute, the shop-girl and slavey. He attempts to achieve what he recognizes in Whitman but only succeeds in displaying his limitations. His Whitmanesque poems contain little significant social comment, for everything is governed by a self too concerned with its own inadequacies to care about anyone else.

The awkward versification of these poems, together with their cloying adolescent mawkishness, obscures the underlying struggle. While there is much pose, there is also much genuine anguish, though the two are often indistinguishable. What indeed may have been Stevenson's tangled emotions at the time too often emerges as a literary attitude in which he plays several roles rather poorly. Yet his attempts to untangle himself are characteristically his own. Beset by a multitude of difficulties, he is torn between an oppressive desire to escape and an equally compelling call to endure. Both are less than satisfactory. A compulsion to escape becomes a need to create sexual fantasy, a crude romance, which is at best temporary. Heroism is likewise suspect. Like many of his later protagonists, his heroism rings false, for its rationale is not so much a meeting of life's challenge as an artful acceptance of inevitability. Perhaps no poem better reveals this dilemma than the "Epistle to Charles Baxter" (Smith, 68), in which he longs to soar if only to fall like Icarus, only to realize that he is not destined to repeat Icarus's "one glorious moment" but his fatal adventure. While still the aspiring creator, he rightly suspects that he may indeed be little more than a skillful imitator embarking on an abortive voyage on which he may "under pleasant fictions bury/ Distasteful truth."

Although the poems in *Underwoods* (1887) are less labored, they express the same tensions as those Stevenson preferred to leave in his notebook. Since they were chosen for publication, they naturally sound the heroic key and accentuate the more strident mannerisms; but their activism is hardly more substantiated than the posturing of the unpublished verse. Activity becomes both means and end. Rather than a measure of experience, it remains a static exercise, a reflex motion which is unthinking and undirected. In those few poems, on the other hand, in which Stevenson mutes his heroics, his conflict becomes sympathetically apparent. Faced with the inescapable urges of his physical being, he details his anxiety with an awkwardness which is charming in its candor. In one poem (Smith, 143), he suggests a fearful contradiction between his body as dungeon and pleasure garden by creating the metaphor of a vast but bound field in which he roams with supposed abandon only to be checked by the elusiveness of his intended freedom. Again, in "Et Tu in Arcadia Vixisti," he celebrates his cousin Bob's ability to deal with the divine and brutal; and he successfully concludes with sadness that in the present world such a reconciliation for him is impossible. Finally, in "A Song of the Road," he sings the very old tune of "over the hills and far away," and embarks upon a lonely journey toward failure.

In the poems written in the South Seas, he speaks clearly about his disillusionment. The pose is gone, and in its place appears a somber moodiness with its memories of friends, places, occasions, now lost except to poetic reminiscence. The final summation appears in "The Woodman." Clearing the jungle for what eventually would be his final home, Stevenson finds himself embattled in a universal struggle for existence; hoping to find a new life, he discovers a Darwinian world in a supposed tropical paradise.

II *Light Verse and Moral Tale*

Like many of his other poems, Stevenson's comic verse is charming and yet unsatisfying.[6] Most of the poems are very much occasional, some prompted by a particular event such as a class reunion; others verse portraits of familiar acquaintances (real and imaginary); burlesque treatments of French and Classical forms; and dedications to friends in return for a gift or merely their friendship. The most interesting are those designated as "Moral Emblems and Tales." [7] The earliest of these were done at the Davos Press before it broke down. [8] Little more than poetic pranks, they are humorous verse equivalents of Stevenson's fables —miniature illustrations of moral lessons with little of the expected sampler mentality. Their major device, as in the fables, is to turn the expected into the unexpected and thus to indicate that indeed "things are seldom what they seem." Two examples: a beau's refusal to dispense charity carries no earthly retribution (one thinks of Beau Austin and John Silver), and murder produces only a mild digestive upset.

As the emblems are to the fables, so are the tales to the longer fiction. Short narrative poems with an appended adage, they were written to be printed at the Davos Press but never went beyond typescript until their publication in the Edinburgh Edition (1898). The first, "Robin and Ben: Or, the Pirate and the Apothecary," is an interesting anticipation of *Treasure Island,* a story of two friends each of whom elects to follow diametrically opposed professions. Robin, after stealing from his mother, runs away to sea, there to become a pirate and to conduct himself with a manliness and honesty not possible had he remained on shore. Ben, his moral opposite, chooses a life of seeming respectability but disguised nefariousness and is mercifully killed by Robin upon his return. The morality turns upon Stevenson's option for an honest rascality above a scheming social obedience.

The second tale, "The Builder's Doom," is again concerned with the possibilities of social duplicity. The chief character, Deacon Thin, a highly respectable member of the community much like Ben, knowingly constructs his tenement buildings with inferior materials and is finally buried under his crumbling workmanship. The moral, however, remains incomplete: the innocent suffer with the guilty; and Deacon Thin, like a perverse Samson, brings down the foundations of his structure upon those who hardly deserve to share his fate. Stevenson's morality is characteristically bitter, for it reflects a realization that the ways of the world are indeed inscrutable. Justice, like virtue, may be a grim reward.

III The Ballads

Perhaps the most surprising omission in Stevenson's ballads is their lack of resemblance to those border ballads so influential on the poets of the early century. In contrast to his conscious imitation of Robert Fergusson and Robert Burns in his Scots poetry, Stevenson in his ballads is content to sound like an unpolished Thomas Macaulay and a diluted Walter Scott.[9] Aware that if the ballads succeeded at all they rested only on their narrative merits (see Letters, IV, 177), Stevenson stopped after writing only three, although he originally planned a volume to consist entirely of ballads (Smith, 491). Unfortunately, even their narrative quality falls short of Stevenson at his best. Generally weighed down by their plodding action and mechanical versification, they are more significant for their relationship to his prose fiction than for their individual merits.

Appropriately, his most successful ballad is most suggestive of his Scottish predecessors. "Ticonderoga: A Legend of the West Highlands" has often been cited for its resemblance to the concluding section of The Master of Ballantrae. Written just after his father's death in 1887, it was probably Stevenson's last composition before permanently leaving Scotland. As such, it contains an amazingly prescient account of a Scotsman who journeys to meet his fate in the wilderness of the New World, a suitable testament to the impossibility of ever escaping one's doom. The story hinges upon divided loyalties—between blood vengeance owed to a brother and a pledge to a guest who has cunningly asked for shelter. Upon a bleak moorland, a Stewart kills a Cameron and then flees to the Cameron's brother, placing himself under the latter's protection. Having faithfully bestowed his hospitality, the dead man's brother can do nothing but deny a call to vengeance. Caught between two rights—honor to family and to guest—and cursed with the haunting death-name of the title, the Cameron goes off to fight his king's battles across the Atlantic and there meets his double and his death.

Simply told and with tight suspense, "Ticonderoga" is Stevenson's most engaging ballad. Like his other compelling characters who must act upon insoluble dilemmas, the Cameron brother is a man doomed to failure whichever way he chooses. His tragedy is built upon an inevitable conflict between two moral positions, a primitive duty to one's blood and a social duty to one's fellow man, each of which is ethically complementary but practically unworkable. Stevenson is fond of placing his characters in exactly such a Hamlet situation, and here he transports his protagonist over the seas in order to indicate, with uncanny anticipation, that the New World may in fact be but the graveyard of the Old.

IV A Child's Garden of Verses

Unlike Stevenson's other poems, *A Child's Garden of Verses* requires little introduction; for, since they were first published in 1885, they have remained a delight to successive generations who hardly know their author's name. Perhaps more listened to than read, and often sung, Stevenson's lyrics play upon the ear with a familiarity which has made them a traditional landmark in growing up/ Recalling meaningful moments of childhood, their wide appeal is not entirely unlike that of Stevenson's other children's literature—*Treasure Island, Black Arrow,* and *Kidnapped*— since all are based upon his belief that "children think very much the same thoughts and dream the same dreams as bearded men and marriageable women" ("Child's Play," II, 124). This belief does not mean that children are merely miniature correspondences of their elders nor that adults conduct their lives with childish anticipation; rather, it indicates that in each life, no matter at what age, there exists some amount of play, some desire to leap over an all-too-pervasive reality into a realm of unlimited possibility. In creating poetry out of his childhood experiences, Stevenson fashions an order of experience whose basis is dream and whose direction is beyond. As the child is to the adult, so too are his compulsions preliminary movements in a never-ending journey out of the self. The poems of childhood are never lost because they are ever repeated. Deservedly the most popular of Stevenson's poems—their verse quality alone insures this—his childhood poems express what his other poems merely suggest, that "In spite of our wisdom/ And sensible talking,/ We on our feet must go/ Plodding and walking" ("Nest Eggs," 400).

Among the memorable qualities of *A Child's Garden of Verses* is the child who "speaks" most of the poems. That he is a child is most important because he speaks to children from their point of view; and, as he speaks with an immediacy unknown in other children's poerty, he imparts a sense of burdensome care and imaginative flight. Not totally identifiable with Stevenson, he nonetheless shares many of his sensibilities. Often alone and lonely, afraid and yet curious of the world about him, frightened by many of its fleeting shadows, longing to travel beyond his limited confines, the child has almost the dimensions of a fictional character lightly sketched in a "narrative" whose line is spiral rather than horizontal.

A child of well-to-do parents, he is cared for by a nurse ("My Kingdom"), and he lives in a large house ("North-West Passage") whose shadows frequently play havoc with his vivid imagination. Though he sometimes plays with others, he is most often dependent upon his own abilities. Usually confined to the walled family garden (even in his one visit to the seashore he is pretty much a solitary reveler), he frequently remains in bed ("The Land of Counterpane"); and he imagines it to be his portal at evening and his haven at morn ("My Bed is a Boat"). Inquisitive as well as introspective, he often thinks of other children either by comparing his daily activities with theirs ("The Sun's Travels") or by sailing his boats down the umbilical river from which "Other little children/ Shall bring my boats ashore" ("Where Go the Boats?"), or by viewing them with a smug self-satisfaction which Stevenson treats with gentle irony ("Foreign Children").

The poems of this sensitive and lonely narrator follow in a familiar and carefully ordered succession.[10] Divided into three sections—the title section contains forty-one poems; nine poems, under the heading "The Child Alone"; and a concluding eight poems, under "Garden Days"—the verses balance each other so that the suggestions of one poem are repeated with slight variation in order to emphasize the constant iteration of like emotion. Accordingly, "The Little Land" of the second section parallels "Foreign Lands" of the first, while "Night and Day" of the third provides a slight but firm echo of both. Again, "Summer Sun" in the concluding section recalls "The Sun's Travels" of the opening part. Occasionally, poems within individual sections compare and contrast with one another. So "My Kingdom" and "The Land of Story-Books" of the third section express the child's isolation in an adult world whose restrictions impair imaginative release, while "Whole Duty of Children" and "System" in the first section reveal the necessary distinction between spiritual will and physical possibility. Similarly, successive poems often reinforce initial attitudes, and so there appear poems on sleep, play, propriety, travel, and nature, each offering its suggestion of unappeasable loneliness.

Not only are the subjects of the poems thus repeated, but identical symbols occur with suggestive frequency. The house, the garden, the wall suggest limitation, something to leave behind or look beyond; darkness, night, the moon, and the wind bring to mind mystery, fright, and an eerie sense of ambiguous freedom. Conversely, the bed, daylight, the swing, the river represent release, the playful leap into the land "where the golden apples grow." By using suggestive imagery, Stevenson is able to maintain and reinforce the alternating emotions of self-centeredness and self-transcendence, the prevailing concordance of childhood delight and simultaneous sadness. Placing his child-narrator in a world from which he is often painfully apart, Stevenson creates a childhood equivalent of universal experience, a miniature gem of Victorian sensibility which speaks pointedly to the isolation of modern life.

Carefully ordered, delicately balanced, intensely subjective, *A Child's Garden of Verses* represents a landmark in children's poetry. Neither didactic nor whimsical, neither Isaac Watts nor Walter De La Mare, Stevenson's poems reconstruct the delicate fancy and persistent longing of children as no other poems have ever done. As a symbol of childhood visions and adult aspirations, Stevenson's child is a dreamer whose dreams constitute a necessity for child and adult alike. Probing his own childhood memories, Stevenson creates a persona who stands midway between childish desire and adult regret; he is a singer of "New Songs of Innocence" (he once thought of using this title) who cautiously anticipates the experience to come.

V *The Scottish Poetry*

Stevenson's Scots poems are most notable for his use of the vernacular, however "synthetic" that use may be.[11] No other Anglo-Scottish writer of the century—neither Scott, Carlyle, Byron, nor John Stuart Mill—chose to reveal so openly his Northern ancestry or to celebrate so declaratively his native tradition.[12] Although Stevenson sustains his poetic limitations in the Scots poems, he nonetheless may claim a legitimate place alongside

Fergusson, Burns and Hugh MacDiarmid. That place, however, can be no more than minor since he shares only a self-conscious nationalism with his two predecessors and their twentieth-century incarnation. Recognized as a major influence on the modern Scottish poets Sydney Smith, Lewis Spence, and MacDiarmid, Stevenson has neither their moral intensity nor their patriotic optimism; viewing himself as the third of the Scottish "Robins," he possesses neither Fergusson's humanism nor Burns's humanity.[13]

Stevenson's Scots and English poems leave little to choose between them. The vernacular provides a sprightly vitality, a pauky humor, and a refreshing objectivity not always present in his other verse, yet even these qualities cannot reclaim the artificiality of "Ille Terrarum," "My Conscience," and "The Maker to Posterity." Even the two long poems, "A Lowden Sabbath Morn," with its distinct echoes of Fergusson and Burns, and "Embro Hie Kirk," a more successful imitation of Fergusson, are literary heirs rather than independent successors. Many of the Scots poems too much resemble the playfulness of his early letters to Baxter, where in the assumed role of Thomson-Johnson they would lapse into the vernacular in order to assert the vitality of two agonizingly Anglified Scotsmen. Game playing is too much the rule, as if Scots could be used for no other purpose than to amuse, as if it could do more than represent the final gasps of a dying culture. In short, Stevenson is too much Harry Lauder and not yet Hugh MacDiarmid.

The appearance of the Scots poems in *Underwoods* (1887), however, after Stevenson had made something of a name for himself, gave them a publicity and a legitimacy beyond his expectations. As verses by an increasingly popular author, they could not be dismissed as mere provincialism. It was his hope that, at best, his readers would consider them as his tribute to the dying Scots tradition. Both the introductory note to the poems and the opening poem itself indicate his belief that he was writing in the last days of his native literature, a literature which could exist only as romance. Expressing a kinship with Fergusson and Burns was his way of indicating that the last days were truly come.

Yet by using Scots, whatever his intention, he proved that the language had more than "A Mile and a Bittock" of literary life remaining. Although his poems display many faults, they are neither sentimental celebrations of "bonnie Scotland" nor tearful regrets at her demise. While not the best of their tradition, they allowed that tradition to continue and to live once again as an instrument of national pride. Not only did these poems enable Stevenson to proclaim his own heritage, but they showed a group of young poets that their native language might be made meaningful in a poetry that could be echoic without being imitative. Stevenson deserves much credit for whatever renaissance Scots poetry has had in the twentieth century. Hoping to maintain his own identity, he wrote better than he knew.

The last sentence may perhaps be considered a suitable comment about all of Stevenson's poetry. Never so skilled nor so careful a craftsman in his verse as in his prose, he had little more than personal pleasure in mind when he scribbled a casual rhyme or a clever imitation. Prose was his medium; and, when he wrote poetry, it was like playing at soldier or like drawing treasure maps for the eager Lloyd. To a point, therefore, a review of his poems reads like a catalogue of verbal toys in which some prove more attractive than others. Stevenson's games, however, are serious; and in his poems he plays with language hoping to find still another voice. Although rarely successful, he occasionally achieved an objective expression beyond the annoying introspection of his early efforts. No better example exists than *A Child's Garden of Verses*. While the child-narrator longs to escape his physical and spiritual prison, his creator has already leapt over the wall of egotism into a world of artistic re-creation.

CHAPTER 5

A Single Glimpse, A Few Sharp Sounds

STEVENSON'S reputation rests on his unquestioned abilities as a storyteller. Working with both short and long fiction, he produced stories and novels that are generally considered to be the creations of a first-rate narrative talent. Stories such as *Jekyll and Hyde* and novels such as *Kidnapped* were immediately able to give him the recognition he sought, and they subsequently kept alive his literary name even when his popularity dimmed. His narrative ability, however, did not always manifest itself equally: too many of his works remain either unrealized or incomplete. In part, this fact must be attributed to uncertain health; in part, to constant travel; in part, to family demands.

But, had he lived a "normal" life, his artistic problems would have still been present. On the simplest level, he faced the difficulty of joining his form to his idea—not only of telling a good story but of insuring that its fictional elements represented the thematic details he wished to communicate. But his well-advertised philosophical position—pessimism in regard to the possibilities of human action—and his well-documented artistic attitude—a belief in the necessity of concision and a minimum of detail—often clashed with his desire to create broadly representative fiction. What he found increasingly was that the didacticism of the essay, the emotion of poetry, and the passion of drama were neither in themselves nor in combination sufficient to create a totally satisfying (even if successful) narrative. His development as a writer is, therefore, a history of repeated attempts to meet the challenge of narrative form.

Stevenson's fictional method is nowhere better described than in his own statement in "A Humble Remonstrance": "Our art is occupied, and bound to be occupied, not so much in making stories true as in making them typical; not so much in capturing the lineaments of each fact, as in marshalling all of them to a common end" (XIII, 150). Consciously placing himself in opposition to Henry James's investigation of "the statics of character," he offers a fiction whose literary relations are allegory, fable, and romance. As distinct as each of these may be in their individual expression, they share an ability to convey the essentials of human experience with a limited intensity which is immediately recognizable: "fear in the single glimpse of an eyeball, evil in a few sharp sounds" (Furnas, 245).

Stevenson creates stories illustrating essential human experience for he wishes to awaken, in both reader and character, those basic internal forces which are called into action only by sufficient external stimuli. These stimuli, activated by a skillful manipulation of extenuating circumstance, force the fictional character to act with a promptness which precludes psychological development while it necessitates that the reader identify fully with the gripping situation. The reader of a Stevenson story can expect to encounter fiction whose spareness is both its virtue and defect, narrative in which characters are "stylized figures which expand into psychological archetypes" (Northrop Frye, *The Anatomy of Criticism* [304]), and plot in which individual detail is clearly, and often conspicuously, joined to final purpose. A typical Stevenson story may be recognized by its blend of myth and melodrama, its normally transparent structure, and its often disappointing conclusion. The disappointment results as much from his hurried attempts to direct events as from his continuing inability to convince himself of the possibilities for action either in art or in experience.

Since Stevenson's short stories were written over a longer period of time—his first story dates from 1877—and are generally more finished than his novels, they provide a more comprehensive view of his fictional method. Published for the most part in separate periodicals, they were subsequently collected under the titles *New Arabian Nights* (1882), *The Merry Men* (1887), and *Island Nights' Entertainments* (1893). The stories in *More New Arabian Nights: The Dynamiter* (1885) were never published separately, are perhaps more Fanny's than her husband's, and are sufficiently similar to the first Arabian stories to be considered along with them.

Conveniently, each of these collections brings together stories of a similar locale and influence so that it is possible to speak of the French stories of *New Arabian Nights*, the Scottish stories of *The Merry Men*, and the South Sea stories of *Island Nights' Entertainments*. In addition, certain stories in each collection may be considered as more or less representative of a characteristic type of Stevenson narrative: in the first, esthetic parody; in the second, psychic fable; and in the third, a special blend of exotic realism. Each collection, therefore, offers a suitable context in which the dimensions of a Stevenson story may be seen in its particular and general relations.

I New Arabian Nights, More New Arabian Nights

Whatever their similarity as early stories, the collected tales of Stevenson's *New Arabian Nights* are separable into related but distinct types: the fictionalized essays of a decided French influence—"A Lodging for the Night," "The Sire de Maletroit's Door," and "Providence and the Guitar"—and the fanciful satires of Victorian England first published as a separate series in Henley's *London Magazine*. The French stories are similar not only because of their obvious influence, but because each employs an elemental fictional technique to illustrate a basic existential necessity.

The first of these, "A Lodging for the Night," reveals its essay origins since it is the direct result of Stevenson's own suggestion in his essay on François Villon that the matter of Villon's thievery could indeed form "a grisly winter's tale." The atmosphere of the story bears out the suggestion; for, not only is the season winter, but every detail in the story assumes a mechanical coldness which reinforces the chill with which humanity is portrayed. Villon's lair is backed against the solitary wall of a snow-covered cemetery, a symbol of the deathlike rigidity which has gripped Medieval Paris. Its inhabitants are creatures of only half a life, a rascally crew reminiscent of the outcasts in *The Ebb-Tide:* a degenerate monk, a debased nobleman, a thorough cutthroat, a fawning imbecile, and a corrupt poet. Each is described not only as a grim specimen but as a totally lost human being. Villon most of all is continually compared to unsavoury animals: the rapacious wolf, the sensual pig, the sneaking cat, and the crafty fox. When one of Villon's minions promptly stabs another during a game of cards, the dead man is dismissed with a galvanic jerk and a sneering bit of spiritual mockery.

A Single Glimpse, A Few Sharp Sounds

Forced to flee the murder scene—Villon hears the rattle of the gibbet upon him—he tracks his way through the empty, snow-covered streets in search of some relief from the bitter cold. Finally, after two refusals, he discovers a house whose "little twinkle of light" suggests the desired possibility; and he begins to close in upon it like an animal about to pounce upon its prey. His intended victim, however, turns out to be an elderly nobleman who teaches him a lesson in conduct and then literally and figuratively dismisses him. Villon finds only temporary lodging, is again forced out into the cold, and must continue his search for shelter to soothe the demands of his parasitical existence.

The story is divided into two distinct sections: a conspicuously symbolic introduction which centers on the gang of thieves, and an expository dialogue between Villon and his temporary host. Such an obvious division in the narrative produces a like division between the fiction and the rhetoric as Stevenson loses faith in his fictional abilities and resorts to the practiced techniques of the essayist. The thematic center of the story is, therefore, not in the fictional details but in the set speeches of Villon and his host amid the aristocratic surroundings so in keeping with their stylized language. As they speak, their roles become extended. Villon is not merely a thief, he is crude, utilitarian man jealous of his place in a Darwinian universe which requires the rapaciousness of his actions. His host, likewise, is not only a former soldier but a figure of heroism who has conducted himself nobly and courageously in the teeth of adversity. Their antithesis, straight out of the essays, is predicated upon necessary conduct within a complex, challenging struggle; and, when the door closes behind Villon, so does all opportunity to save himself. If anything, the door is too firmly shut; and, though Villon may attempt to comfort himself with a shrugging dismissal, the reader remains uncomfortable in his realization that the story has produced little more than a confirmation of Stevenson's previous description of Villon in "François Villon: Student, Poet, and Housebreaker" as "a sinister dog . . . [with] an overweening sensual temperament. . . . Certainly the sorriest figure in the rolls of Fame." (V, 171.)

The closed door which marks Villon's final dismissal opens upon Denis de Beaulieu's adventure and thrusts him into a life-death challenge. This parallel, among others, suggests that the story of "The Sire de Maletroit's Door" should be read as a complement to Villon's experience. In addition to certain stylistic similarities—verbal embroidery, heavily symbolic physical details, consciously didactic conversations—the entire narrative structure resembles the direction of Villon's movements through the somber Parisian streets. While the time is autumn rather than winter, the streets are no less dangerous.

Denis, a French soldier in the war between his country and the English, depends upon the fragile security of his safe-conduct pass to keep him from the clutches of the watch. Intent on a visit (is there a hint of assignation?), he is noticed and chased until his only retreat is a hastily opened door through which he plunges into a spare but clearly aristocratic chamber. Here he meets the Sire de Maletroit and his niece-ward Blanche and is mistaken for Blanche's supposed lover who presumably has compromised her reputation. Faced with the choice of marriage or death, Denis wisely chooses the former, but only after he assures Blanche that his choice is prompted by a nobility which teaches that any life is to be preferred before the stark reality of a death where "a man gets into his tomb and has the door shut after him till the judgement day."

The narrative action presents a brief, elaborate charade in which the characters are meant to act out a paradigm of heroic experience. Provided with a safe-conduct whose utility is challenged by every chance encounter, man is constantly forced to meet circumstance with an immediacy necessitating a choice much like Denis's. Unfortunately, the fiction is again obvious and insufficient. While the original "mousetrap" in the title was replaced by the less melodramatic "door," the details are blocked out with an inflexibility which betrays Stevenson's uncertain hand. *Beau-lieu* (fair place), the fair, handsome, delicately feminine soldier, and *Mal-etroit* (evil(ly)-narrow), the grossly masculine, seedy nobleman are as obviously opposed as Villon and his host. Blanche, as both her name and person suggest, is too "white" to be believable, while the choice she presents, a variant of the beauty-beast legend, is not sufficiently challenging to be effective. The result is an intriguing paradox: a cameo etched so exquisitely that each intricate detail becomes more attractive than the whole.

In "Providence and the Guitar," Stevenson begins to use his

fiction more flexibly and more fully. Still too much a representation of a philosophical attitude, the story nonetheless contains the beginnings of fictional characterization in Monsieur Léon Berthelini. An actor, musician, composer, and dandy, Monsieur Léon is woefully unsuccessful in all his enterprises. He instinctively recognizes, however, that he must continue to "act" despite failure, to affect the pose of freedom in order to withstand the finality of despair. His act and his action are one, and the measure of his being is in the doing, not in its invariably unsuccessful result. Unlike Villon or Denis, he is no longer a symbolic static figure. His actions are self-motivated and part of a fictional context whose details are not quite so self-consciously balanced. In fact, the story rambles in a strangely pleasing and realistic way. If "Providence and the Guitar" is less thematically intelligible, it is better fiction than the more essaylike stories, a glimpse into the bohemian life which allows the reader to take what he will but which does not force him to take anything more than amusement.

The charming playfulness which makes "Providence and the Guitar" such a pleasant gambol turns the tales of the *New Arabian Nights* more toward apparent confusion than intended amusement.[1] Stevenson's most ambitious fiction to date, these stories play havoc with some of the most pressing contemporary (and human) problems and have no doubt perplexed more readers than they have entertained. Not until Robert Kiely's book had anyone seen them as necessary for Stevenson's development as a writer of fiction; and, though Kiely's view is limited, his critical suggestions are invaluable. He understands that these stories must be read as Stevensonian comedy. Accordingly, he identifies them as comic satire and discusses both their initial satiric success and their eventual inconclusive failure. They fail, Kiely contends, because Stevenson set out to write satire, which he achieved in "The Suicide Club," but soon descended into "the protective excesses of farce and melodrama" (120). Kiely fails to consider, however, that both the parodic title and the varied style suggest that no one form of comedy may be sufficient to describe all of the collected tales, and that both farce and melodrama may, in fact, be integral devices.[2]

As "New Arabian Nights," the stories are intentionally modeled on those fantastic tales which by Stevenson's time had become a standard part of every Victorian library.[3] Like the earlier tales, these are strung together loosely around a reappearing monarchical character who in Stevenson's version is a combination of Haroun Al Raschid and the Prince of Wales.[4] Such a structure insures that fictional continuity will be due more to the presence of his narrative character than to any particular stylistic or thematic identity. Although satire may be the dominant mode of the first story, it is appropriate that later stories develop other forms of comedy. The change in comic forms is necessary because, in writing a parody of *The Arabian Nights*, Stevenson was clearly attempting to emulate their variety as well as imitate their comic powers. By invoking the imaginative fantasy of *The Arabian Nights*, he hoped to fashion a romantically comic world which could be insubstantial while still relevant. As often, he hoped for more than he achieved.

That Stevenson was not constitutionally disposed to be a satirist was clear as early as 1870 when, in the sketch, "A Satirist," he revealed an inability to castigate with a necessary unmerciful venom. Unwilling to present only one side, he was equally unable to accept the possibility which the alternative view implied. A disbeliever in the possibility of successful completion, he could not take seriously the reformative posture which satire requires. Thus whenever he attempted to write satire—"Robin and Ben," for example—he achieved only the hollowness of exposé and soon abandoned the form as unsatisfying. The satire in *New Arabian Nights* must be read as part of the total comedy, for it is only as part of an unchanging world that Stevenson's satire exists.

The comedy which informs *New Arabian Nights* joins with the given exoticism of the traditional stories to create a world both less and more real than the actual. The combination creates a humorous equivalent of Victorian England in which men and manners are turned topsy-turvy and irony gives way to whimsy. In a study of *The Arabian Nights*, Margaret Annan points out some of the Stevensonian reversals that produce this comic travesty: wonder becomes melodrama, exotic Arabia gives way to familiar London, murder replaces love as the mode of intrigue, and death, not life, is the final reward. Such reversals do much to relate Stevenson's stories to their source and to broaden their comic reflections on British society. But for Stevenson there are additional inversions necessary. These play not so much upon a particular model as upon popular motifs found in all literature. Their purpose is to place Stevenson's stories in an identifiable literary tradition and to strengthen the meaning of his comedy. In "The Suicide Club," the traditional search for escape becomes a quest for death; in "The Story of the Physician and the Saratoga Trunk," the trunk and the corpse it holds becomes a material equivalent of original sin which man can no more easily discard than Silas can rid himself of his burden; and in "The Rajah's Diamond," fabulous riches become an impediment rather than a means to pleasure. Stevensonian comedy is adventure reversed because it emphasizes man's inability to overcome his limitations. Although circumstance remains a challenge, man's greatest challenge is his ineffectual self. Such comedy requires farce as well as satire since man is constantly reminded of his physical limitations within a frenetic, uncontrollable world. Satire and farce are allies in a comic world which begins as satiric reform but ends as farcical acceptance.

The first series of stories in *New Arabian Nights*, "The Suicide Club," concerns the adventures of Prince Florizel and his companion, Colonel Geraldine, with the jaded, cowardly members of a club dedicated to effortless self-destruction. Their guide to this society of decadent misfits is a young man (modeled upon Stevenson's cousin, Robert Mowbray Stevenson) whose disillusionment with life is symbolized in his reduction of all its challenges to the successive devouring of several cream tarts. Dissatisfied with his briefly satisfying prank, he decides to play cards with his life and conducts his new acquaintances to Victorian England at the end of its tether. For that is what the suicide club amounts to: its inhabitants, most of whom are "in the prime of youth," personify the malaise which has gripped the age; they form a microcosm of *fin de siècle* England gambling away its youth and its future.

Among them, two members serve as contrasts: the president of the club and Mr. Malthus, its honorary member. Appropriately, neither is young. The first is a Machiavelli thriving on others' misery. The dealer in a game in which only death is the winner, he is a vivid example of age's exploitation of youth's follies, a pimp whose product is easeful death, "from hope and fear set free." Mr. Malthus, as his name pointedly suggests, is an amoral monster who looks upon life from his confining wheelchair as a voyeur through a titillating crack in the wall (Silas Q. Scudda-more in the next story has similar tendencies), afraid to partake of its dangers but anxious to be thrilled by its nakedness. A cow-ard, which he proudly considers the height of dissipation, Mal-thus finally toys with death too triflingly and meets it with a horrible scream, as "the noise of his bones upon the pavement" echoes the empty skeleton that he has always been.

The satire is clear. Stevenson is mocking his effete, passive con-temporaries, of which certain artists are only the most obvious examples. Yet from its very beginning the satire lacks necessary bite. Introduced by a whimsical prank, continued in a symbolic location midway between fantasy and reality, it finally depends upon melodrama to maintain its contact with actuality. Only when Florizel is himself threatened with death does the reader feel that the actions before him have any relation to reality, and the reality is not a choice of a way of life but of life itself. By the time Florizel is saved through Geraldine's intervention, the chance for satiric ridicule is gone. The final two episodes conjure up a fantastic setting in which any action is outwardly farcical and ultimately false.

The scene of the next episode, "The Story of the Physician and the Saratoga Trunk," shifts between Paris and London but specific location is unimportant. Its action, insignificant in itself, concerns the death of Colonel Geraldine's brother at the hands of the president of the Suicide Club. The central character is Silas Q. Scuddamore, whose exploits are those of a Mr. Malthus with the monstrousness become buffoonery. A young American of modest abilities but marked curiosity, he is lured into conspiring with villains by his habitual voyeurism. Neighbor to a woman whose charms he is fond of observing through a hole in the wall, he becomes an unwilling accomplice in the transportation of Colonel Geraldine's dead brother back to England.

This central action gives the story its narrative being and the-matic substance. The trunk's contents are immaterial, but Silas's bungling attempts to remove a literal burden from his unwilling shoulders is a classic illustration of the myth of Sisyphus reduced to a mundane equivalent. The ensuing action is broadly farcical. Silas juggles the overweight trunk between its intended destina-tion and his own rooms as if it were both more fragile and more significant than it actually is. Like a hero of twentieth-century fiction, he is a little man forced to perform an insignificant yet hazardous action in a world this side of absurdity. Farce conditions the absurd by implying that some order remains, yet its assurances are less than satisfying. There is not even the customary romantic plot which lightens its anarchistic mayhem. Instead, Silas returns to America there to seek—and gain—political glory while the scheming murderer is propelled to his final confrontation with Prince Florizel.

The final episode, "The Adventure of the Hansom Cab," carries insubstantiality one step further. Moving toward the death of the Suicide Club's president, it turns instead upon the method of selection for Florizel's seconds. In an opening scene, meant as a parody of the Suicide Club itself, Lieutenant Brackenbury Rich, just returned to London from serving in India, is conveyed to a luxuriously appointed house which he takes to be a gambling den. Much to his surprise, guests continue to drop away as the evening progresses; and, when he steps into the hall, he is astounded to see that all the furniture is gone. It has all been a trick of Geraldine's to select the right man to serve with his Prince; but, when the time comes for heroics, Lieutenant Rich is again left behind in still another empty mansion. Substance becomes sham and melodrama comedy as the stories change from satire to melodrama to farce to fantasy.

The entire adventure is little more than a trick, and the Suicide Club itself is merely a stage setting of cardboard flat and painted tableau. "Thus even the most serious concerns," says Geraldine, "have a merry side," and the stories of "The Suicide Club" highlight that merriment as a corollary of the serious. In fact, the serious can only be saved from a fatal seriousness when tempered by the comic. If the world of "The Suicide Club" is not much more than a pack of cards, the players still hope to avoid the ace of spades. They can either trust to chance, or throw themselves upon "the great battlefield of mankind," even while suspecting that their actions are but gestures in a make-believe world.

In the stories of "The Rajah's Diamond," Prince Florizel begins his descent from the throne by fading into the background, removing not only his cohesive presence but also the necessary melodramatic attraction. Without Prince Florizel and his intrigues, the stories hang together only on the slender thread of parody and fantasy. The central parodic device is the rajah's diamond, the rich but destructive jewel of the East; and the parody is not only of the myth of the treasure hunt, but most directly of Wilkie Collins's *The Moonstone*. As the diamond is passed from character to character, many types of Englishmen are ridiculed: Harry Hartley, the feminine man; Rolles, the materialistic clergyman; John Vandeleur, the incorrigible imperialist; and Francis Scrymegeour, the well-meaning muddler. While presenting these varied characters, Stevenson also takes great delight in laughing at some of the more popular literary affectations: the worship of materialism, the bisexual male, and the search for a lost father and a legitimate identity. Each of these is touched on lightly and then allowed to dissolve into the gossamer of the fantastic. Given little of substance, the reader must agree to be either dazzled or bored. Eventually, the artistic splendor of the stories, like the diamond which figures in each of them, proves destructive.

Even Prince Florizel's reduction from monarch to tobacconist, which otherwise might have been a witty gibe at the woes of modern rulers ("We should all be as happy as kings"), is lost in the surfeit of whimsical contrivance. Though Florizel actually becomes Theophilus Godall (only a disguise previously), he, like his hypothetical Arabian author, might as well have been sent "topsy-turvy into space." At the end of his adventures in *New Arabian Nights*, he exists with as little substance as the disbanded Suicide Club or the irretrievable Rajah's diamond. From playing at omniscient and omnipotent god, he becomes an insignificant member of a nation of shopkeepers.

Stevenson's direction toward pure fantasy is more pronounced but less manageable in *The Dynamiter* stories. Planned as a continuation of *New Arabian Nights*, they have only a tangential relationship to their predecessors, linked at best by the pale figure of Florizel-Godall. Whether one believes that they were written mostly by Fanny and perhaps revised by Stevenson, or that they are only Stevenson's, their comedy is necessarily more forced and less laughable. Begun in 1883 at Hyères, the stories refer directly to the series of Fenian dynamite plots which terrorized the large cities of England that year.[5] If historical accounts are accurate, few Englishmen took the bombings lightly; and Stevenson himself, in his dedication to the stories, cites the two policemen who

apparently helped save London from damage, Officers Cole and
Cox, as worthy of standing alongside the martyred General Gordon.[6] Thus the threatening presence of the real makes it ex-
tremely difficult to transform it into fantasy, especially when the
author (?) of that fantasy only half believes in its attraction.

In *The Dynamiter*, all of life and art is a bubble which bursts
with a suddenness meant to elicit equally sudden laughter. Yet if
laughter is an antidote against the destructive mindlessness which
the anarchists represent—see "The Day After To-Morrow" (II,
248)—it rings as hollow as that which accompanies Challoner as
he goes off on his fool's errand. Each of the interlocking stories—
that of the Mormons which so fascinated Conan Doyle he used
it in *A Study in Scarlet*, or that of the Fair Cuban with its evoca-
tive but fabricated suggestions of voodoo and cannibalism—is
ultimately revealed to be false, and the anarchist women to be
more adept at storytelling than their men at producing effective
bombs.

The classic illustration of the anarchist's bungling harmlessness
is "Zero's Tale of the Explosive Bomb," the one story almost all
agree was written by Stevenson. It concerns an attempted bomb-
ing of Shakespeare's statue in Leicester Square. The plot is foiled,
however, and the cowardly bomber wanders about London attempting to dispose of the box which contains the already-trig-
gered mechanism. Like Silas Scuddamore, he is chained to an
inescapable burden, this time of his own manufacture. Finding it
impossible to dispose of his bag—he tries little girls, stray women,
hansom drivers—he finally tosses it into the Thames and plunges
in after it. Saved from death by the ubiquitous Godall, he
emerges from the river only to see the bomb explode in a wet
gurgle. The bomb's final impact is much like the collections':
"a dull and choked explosion shook the solid masonry of the
Embankment, and far out in the river a momentary fountain rose
and disappeared."

The stories of *New Arabian Nights* and *The Dynamiter* are
for the most part entertaining examples of Stevenson's groping
toward a new literary direction. Having begun as an essayist, he
found himself most comfortable with fictional exposition, and his
early stories are written very much in this mode. They have about
them the coldness of rational discourse and the mechanical rigid-

ity of their inspiration. The Arabian Nights stories, on the other hand, break away from this structure. Inspired by a literature that is the antithesis of clarity and careful plotting, Stevenson adopts the artistic brilliance and intrinsic insubstantiality of his model and adapts them to fit a world in difficulty if not decline. He takes from *The Arabian Nights* their mixture of comedy and melodrama, and their casual ability to laugh at the most serious of life's dilemmas. At times, as in *The Dynamiter* stories, he tries too hard to emulate them and achieves only a weak imitation; at other moments, as in "The Suicide Club," he succeeds in creating a skillful parody which may be considered a legitimate parallel. Most of all, he conveys his immense delight at *The Arabian Nights* tales while he uses them to develop his fictional voice.

II The Merry Men

Stevenson's development as a short-story writer, however, cannot be measured linearly. Always some residue remains of past influence and unaccomplished intention. In his next collection, *The Merry Men*, two of the stories, "Will O' The Mill" and "The Treasure of Franchard," are a look backward; both are allegories whose artistry beckons with an awkward charm. The first is an idyll about the reclusive life which Stevenson felt emotionally attractive but intellectually abhorrent, and David Daiches correctly finds that the atmosphere jars with the intended allegory (12). It is the disparity found in the essays, where didactic purpose and ambivalent conclusions are not unexpected.

"The Treasure of Franchard" is a more developed story and a less effective allegory. As its name implies, it is still another variation on Stevenson's favorite treasure theme,[7] one written at approximately the same time as *Treasure Island*. As allegory, it attempts to depict both the charms of the Grez countryside and the destructive lure of unearned wealth. As narrative, it attempts to add motivation and characterization to direct presentation. The combination is awkward, although instructive, for it allows Stevenson to extend his intentions even at the cost of his story. As in "Will O' The Mill," the allegory fades into the scenery, and the scenery becomes more memorable than any intended didacticism. Likewise, the characters of Dr. Desprez and Jean-Marie transcend whatever ideas they are supposed to represent, and the entire story may indeed be read as "a rather charming study of

French provincial life at its most attractive . . ." (Daiches, 14).

While Stevenson never entirely abandoned allegory, it became less a form and more an integral device in his subsequent fiction. The combination, dissonant in "The Treasure of Franchard," became less so as Stevenson grew more skillful in narrative blending. This is certainly true of the remaining stories in the collection, stories which represent some of Stevenson's most original contributions to fiction. In them, he begins to focus upon his psychological interests and upon the literary traditions of his native country. The first interest leads him to the creation of psychic fables, stories which reveal his Calvinist background; the second allows him to work with the traditional ghost story, developing it from a crude thriller ("The Body Snatcher") into imaginative symbolic supernaturalism ("The Merry Men").

In a letter to Lady Taylor, written about a year after the publication of "Markheim" and "Olalla," (January, 1887), Stevenson compares them and complains that "*Markheim* is true; *Olalla* false; and I don't know why, nor did I feel it when I worked at them; indeed I had more inspiration with *Olalla* as the style shows" (Letters, II, 327). The trouble with "Olalla" is that *too much* of the style shows. Stevenson's comparison implies that both stories were written as psychic fables, attempted depictions of man's battle with the cosmic and the personal forces which challenge his being. Where "Markheim," however, uses its symbolic suggestions with telling success, "Olalla" attempts to emerge unblemished from an unstable combination of Scotland and Spain, Calvinism and Catholicism, but succeeds only in achieving "a cardboard Spanish setting and preposterously artificial action . . ." (Daiches, 15). "Olalla" is undeniably artificial, yet its depiction of malignant atavism remains strangely fascinating. The seduction of the muleteer, the blood lust of the Senora, and the final parting of the narrator and the title character are among the most powerful scenes Stevenson wrote. Furthermore, his portrayal of the human animal in its successive stages of decay is a chilling record of inherent brutality and its inescapable retention even unto the end of days.

In a plot that is deceptively simple, a wounded Scottish soldier, having fought in the Continental wars, is sent into the Spanish mountains to recuperate. He is housed with a family of decaying nobility and warned not to become too friendly with his hosts. When he meets them, however, he is intrigued by the apparent disparity between their physical beauty and their brutal behavior. In each of the three members of the family—the aging but still beautiful Senora whose gaze is a vegetable blankness; her son, Felipe, the feline innocent who is more nature's creature than man's; and her daughter, Olalla, the willful penitent afraid to face her own destiny—he finds alternating attraction and repulsion until he is forced to deny not only them but much of himself. As his attraction grows into seeming love for Olalla, he becomes increasingly fearful of his own animalistic potential. Driven away finally by a manifestation of the family's bestiality—the Senora excitedly bites an open wound upon his hand—he retreats from a challenge which he finds himself too much of a "romanticizer" to meet effectively. Unable to love, he can only leave Olalla to the martyred Christ. A tearful penitent in a life of chosen resignation, she remains to embrace statues instead of life.

Such a straightforward plot deserves obvious symbols. Thus, the blood metaphor obtrudes markedly throughout the story. As the Senora's family is a partial microcosm of the human family—mother, son, daughter—so their blood links them not only to their respective bestial relations but to all other humans of whom they are crude examples. When the narrator is sent into the mountains —an obvious symbol of the other side of civilization—he is told that the natural air will renew his blood; and, subsequently, when he attempts to deny the truth about himself and Olalla, it is after the Senora has made their "blood" relationship undeniably apparent. Finally, the image of Christ with which the story concludes, is that of a bleeding martyr with a "ghastly, daubed countenance" and "painted wounds." Blood is not only the prerequisite for life but the link between barbarism and civilization, the source of man's being and the reminder of his brutality. Both Olalla and the soldier fear their blood, and both forego its regenerative powers in order to sacrifice themselves.

If plot and symbol are rather crudely obvious, much remains in the story that either is not fully realized or is purposely ambiguous. Why the Spanish setting, for example, or the opposition between Catholicism and Calvinism? Stevenson could have chosen a primitive location with which he was more familiar; and, while Olalla's Catholicism is heavily pronounced, the narrator's Calvinism is suggested so lightly that it seems hardly a parallel or an alternative. Even the portrayal of familial decay is more striking than convincing. The greatest difficulty, however, occurs in the final scene. Surely the narrator and Olalla have chosen wrongly, surely the choice is contrary to Stevenson's belief, surely Christ's sacrifice need not be man's; but ambiguities remain.

Even the final "sermon" delivered by the narrator is filled with uncertainties terminated by a (consciously?) perplexing pun: "that it is best to suffer all things and do well." One can suffer like Olalla and embrace martyrdom or suffer the "slings and arrows of outrageous fortune" and continue to endure (to add to the complexity, Olalla just before asked the soldier to "Suffer me to pass on my way alone"). Perhaps all meanings are intended. Yet above all towers the crowning figure of the martyred Christ, and the uncertain yet necessary relationship between his sacrifice and the creature for whom that sacrifice was made. In "Olalla," Stevenson seemingly intends to contrast Christ's sacrifice and man's. Jesus gave of himself so that man may accept all of life, even with its contradictions. In refusing to accept life, the soldier and Olalla deny their past and future.

"Olalla" is all its critics say it is—crude, artificial, unrealized—yet it remains a haunting narrative of inescapable atavism in a Darwinian world having to make sense of its reality. Among Stevenson's fiction, it is a striking but abortive example of the necessary concern for "Probably Arboreal." [8] Like that player in the Suicide Club who "could not bear to be descended from an ape," the people of "Olalla" choose to retreat from the challenge of an uncertain destiny.

While the reaction to "Markheim" has been more favorable than to "Olalla," the difficulties it presents may be seen even in those who consider it successful. The major difficulty centers around the role of the visitant and the contradictory attempts to identify that hallucinatory being with absolute moral equivalents. For some, he is an angel; for others, the devil; but the more cautious prefer a psychological identity to a qualitative label. Even those critics who replace much of the confusion with a discussion of Stevenson's imaginative use of symbol and literary allusion are overly concerned with reading the narrative as a record of "a sinner's progress." [9] But the symbolic structure which they document forbids such analysis and reinforces the ambiguities which make "Markheim" a moral fable without a moral. The story's action is markedly interior; and, as that action passes from the stylized antique shop of the murdered dealer to the increasingly frenzied mind of the murderer, external objects—clocks, footsteps, mirrors, raindrops—begin to assume the subjective murkiness of Markheim's guilt-ridden ego. In fact, much in the story recalls both Dostoevsky and Nabokov, especially the climatic confrontation of a hapless being with his compulsive double identity.[10]

Stevenson's fiction never approaches the involved complexity nor the moral intensity which both Dostoevsky and Nabokov fashion so ingeniously. Yet he, like them, admires and follows the *Doppelganger* tradition and its use of doubles to suggest tormented psychology.[11] While the respective doubles assume various forms, they are usually projections of subconscious drives personified in an alter-ego which forces its counterpart into unwilling action and eventual death. A man's double is a manifestation of hidden or disguised truths which have been willfully submerged. Stevenson's creation of a double in his story suggests that Markheim's identity must be defined rather than the visitant's, for the visitant is a product of Markheim's deranged mind or of his long-dormant conscience. Whatever the visitant is, therefore, it has no objective reality; it attains form and meaning only as Markheim acts and reflects upon his actions. Because its origin is an unwilling summons from an unknown self, it is able to disguise its true motives and direct Markheim into an unwilling act of surrender. The final irony occurs when Markheim disobeys what he believes to be its promptings and surrenders himself to the police. Summoned by a senseless murder, the visitant leaves only when certain that the murderer will pay for his act. With an obvious reversal of the Christmas setting and its significance, the materialized conscience demands suicide for a life of crime.

A psychology which creates an ambiguous alter-ego cannot be considered as either good or evil. Markheim's actions substantiate the complicated emotions which trouble him. At the point of killing the dealer, he still wishes for some saving grace to stay his hand; and, when he stoops over the prostrate heap that was a man, he thinks back upon his religious training and the domestic comforts he knew as a boy. While a sinner, he has suffered immeasurably by his plunge into the irreversible paradigm of criminal action. Hesitant at the outset, he allows his qualms only a partial voice for fear that he will have to face the truth about himself. Now that his actions have led him to murder—"All sinful acts run to murder. Murder is a distinction without a difference" ("The Ethics of Crime," II, 209)—he has no choice but to cease his action. What he must atone for, more than the murder itself, is his existence as a moral coward. An equivocator, he is afraid to look at himself when presented with the reality which his subconscious no longer allows him to deny. Before he meets his double, he shuns the candlelight, refuses to look at himself in the mirror, and wishes to throw himself under the bedcovers where he may be "invisible to all but God." He fears God less than man because he believes his justification sufficient; but, knowing he has wronged man, he cowers before the truths which self-examination reveals. More pitiful than tragic, he is a lost soul who can "save" whatever remains of his life only by ending it.

Both narrative structure and symbolic pattern help to reveal Markheim's involved psychology. The murder is made to appear a senseless act without purpose. Initially, he performs the killing mechanically as if someone else were guiding the dagger in his hand; only after he has killed the dealer does he consider taking his money. Having murdered, he shies away from his act in fear: fear of the crumpled body and of the shadows which seem to remind him of the inescapable actuality of his act. As he flees the murder room and retreats to an upper story of the dealer's house, these shadows pursue him until they begin to form themselves into alternating configurations of his own guilt and the dealer's accusing image. Left with no escape, he shudders convulsively when he hears steps upon the landing and barely stifles a scream when the door opens upon his double.

In their subsequent conversation, Markheim refuses the "evil" counsel which he believes his double offers, yet his refusal is less than complete. More conscious than his actions reveal or than he would admit, he has always shied away from responsibility; eager to satisfy his desires ("I would not hurry away from any pleasure"), he has willingly allowed self-indulgence to become a way of life. As a result, his final surrender is more an act of resignation than of salvation. He gives himself up to the police with the same spirit that Olalla returns to her cloister; afraid to face his existence—he reviews his life as "a scene of defeat"—he embraces the opportunity to end it: "Life . . . tempted him no longer; but on the further side he perceived a quiet haven for his bark."

The image of a boat coming to its final rest is suggestive of the poems in *A Child's Garden of Verses* in which the child longs for some respite from his oppressive world. Like that child, Markheim directs his life toward ultimate negation; and his final act may be seen as a grim, adult parallel of the sentiments in "My Bed is Like a Little Boat." Unlike that child, however, Markheim is a trifler with life; and the fantasy of his thirty-six-year existence can no longer be played beneath the bedcovers. Time has caught up with him. Its symbolic and actual presence in the story emphasizes his defeat even as it beats like the throbbing of his jangled emotions until he can no longer deny its finality.

First there is the actual narrative time and the necessary telescoping of events in order to highlight Markheim's increasing mental instability. Second, there are the artifacts of measurable time, most notably the antique clocks which chime the final hours of his indecision. Since they are antique clocks they are, as it were, double indicators of time's relentless pursuit: both in their age and function they confront Markheim with his inescapable guilt. Imprisoned by time and its artifacts, he signals his growing frenzy by internalizing other sounds as time's reminders: church bells which ring in the hour of three; raindrops which beat like the ticking of clocks. Time and circumstance meet, and Markheim can deny neither. Having already offered poverty and "the giants of circumstance" as excuses, he has no choice but to confess his guilt and accept his surrender: "If I be condemned to evil acts . . . there is still one door of freedom open—I can cease from action. If my life be an ill thing, I can lay it down." Placed before the familiar Stevenson door of opportunity, he chooses to close it upon a wasted existence.

Markheim's final decision is meant to be difficult since it is between surrender or another murder, and its ambiguities are compounded by the story's Christmas setting. Made to resemble Christian resignation, his passive act is nonetheless as much a denial of Christ's sacrifice as Olalla's was. Coupled with the visitant's rather primitive demand of his life for the one he has taken, it is a striking illustration of the inevitability of failure. It is also a glaring example of the doubts that Stevenson had about the possibility of salvation; for, in "A Christmas Sermon" he writes of the necessity to persevere despite uncertainties he could never deny. The heroic in life, he says, is "to co-endure with our existence." At Christmas, the conclusion of another year, man is called to self-examination; at the end of present time he must account for his past actions. Markheim likewise is forced to consider how he has spent his own time, and he must acknowledge that both its physical and spiritual dimensions offer only one solution; inextricably bound to the consequences of sinful action and cowardice, he can do nothing but stop time. Unlike the ideal man of Stevenson's essay, Markheim can take comfort from neither life nor death. His final act saves the life of the returning maid but condemns his own guilty existence. In doing so, he insures his actions will cease, while death remains a mystery. His surrender is neither good nor evil; it is only the end of an unrealized life—a conclusion without consolation.

In contrast to the other narratives in *The Merry Men*, Stevenson's Scottish stories are firmly localized, often with such overt particularity that their intended symbolism becomes obscured. Stevenson's comment that "Thrawn Janet" was "true only historically . . . not true for mankind and the world," might apply to the title story as well. Both stories exhibit his use of Scottish folklore as a symbolic configuration capable of revealing universal truth while retaining particular application. This double vision occasionally results in a sacrifice of both intentions: the heavy use of Scottish speech and setting puts too much emphasis on the particular, while the hurried leap to the symbolic leaves the individual details connected tenuously to their national origins.

Stevenson's use of Scotland as a meaningful fictional setting develops slowly from its early appearance in "The Pavilion on the Links" (1879). *Kidnapped* (1886) represents his first successful union of setting and theme, but he achieves total integration only in the unfinished *Weir of Hermiston*. In the early stories, he is intent upon establishing identifiable norms, so that, although the Berwick coast is appropriate to the bleak atmosphere of "Pavilion on the Links," it matters little that it is a Scottish wasteland. Similarly, the plot of "The Body Snatcher" is based upon the resurrectionist activities of Burke and Hare, legendary Scottish grave robbers; but the Edinburgh setting is little more than standard atmospherics. Only in "The Misadventures of John Nicholson" (1887) is there a synthesis characteristic of Stevenson's best Scottish stories. As uneven as the story may be, it belongs nowhere but in Edinburgh; for Stevenson seems clearly to be writing out of his own frustrations with a city with which he could never make final peace. Not only is John Nicholson's father much like his own, but every detail in the story—place names, domestic situations, historical allusions—is fully understandable only through a knowledge of their Scottish context. Stevenson develops his use of Scotland as he begins to incorporate its richness more organically into his fiction.

"Thrawn Janet" and "The Merry Men" stand between superficial recollection and the conscious echo of national epic. More provincial than epic, they combine setting, language, and myth to present a powerful though limited picture of man's tortured soul. Paradoxically, both their power and their limitation depend upon their close imitation of Scottish speech and their use as central myth of the legendary belief in the devil as a black man. While the approximation of Scottish vernacular adds authenticity, the broad Scots, particularly in "Thrawn Janet," creates difficult reading and a somewhat narrow focus. Likewise, although the myth of the black man provides a highly suggestive symbolic apparatus, it allows Stevenson to substitute superstitious horror for moral investigation. In both stories, history exists more as personal narrative than as a varied series of complex events in which the individual must affirm his role.

The setting of "Thrawn Janet" is obviously symbolic. Although many of its place names exist in scattered parts of Scotland, they are brought together in order to create an ominous landscape: the parish of Balweary in the Vale of Dule, the Hanging Shaws, the Dei'l's Hag, Black Hill, and Knockdaw (gloomy hill). These suggestions of foreboding are enhanced by the fiercely compelling narrator who, like a latter-day Ancient Mariner, fixes one to his story with a magnetic style, if not with a "glittering eye." His story is concerned with conversion from rational skepticism to superstitious credulity. The Reverend Murdoch Soulis, who comes to Balweary fresh out of college, proceeds to certify the towns-people's suspicions by employing as his housekeeper a well-known sinner who is suspected of being a witch. He continues to defy the townspeople on her behalf even after her sly renun-ciation of the devil and after her subsequent affliction with a crooked neck and incomprehensible speech. Unaware of these signs of her possession, Reverend Soulis continues in his skepti-cism until he is confronted first by the apparition of her limp body hanging upon a nail and then by the devil's pursuit in her lifeless form. Frightened beyond unbelief, he condemns both master and maid to hell and himself to a worship of what his favorite sermon text calls "the devil as a roaring lion."

The pattern of conversion is marked, but it is also perverse. Reverend Soulis goes from rational hesitancy to zealous accep-tance, from a center of indifference to an everlasting yea. Yet the ethical direction of his affirmation is disturbingly negative since his belief is neither toward God nor himself, but toward Satan; and it serves to confirm him only as a devil worshipper. He thus reverses the meaning of Teufelsdrockh's paradigm and changes himself from a naive, gifted young clergyman into a frightening incarnation of Satanic possession. Once again, Stevenson's skep-ticism is manifest. Hardened to a fixed position, Reverend Soulis turns to its antithesis when confronted by an experience he can-not explain. In doing so, he proves that possession can be both symbolic and real and that its true horror is seen when supersti-tion becomes belief.

Despite its brilliance, "Thrawn Janet" remains too much a "crawler"; and the story is saved from being only that by Steven-son's skillful handling of dialect and detail. In comparison, "The Merry Men" is a highly developed narrative; as Stevenson him-self said, "It is, I fancy, my first real shoot at a story" (Letters, II, 43). As a first attempt at a rounded narrative, it succeeds tentatively; and, although certain effects are unrealized, its depic-tion of man and nature in conflict is memorable. Stevenson's un-certainty is apparent: he uses the familiar treasure hunt in order to generate action, barely disguises the terrain of the islet of Earraid, introduces undeveloped religious symbols in order to raise the story to cosmic significance, and hints at a murder whose function is more literary than ethical. His highest achievement, however, is indicative of his maturing talent: Gordon Darnaway is an impressive figure of Godly defiance whose ambivalence toward an awesome nature is that of Victorian man in a world which offers little comfort and no cheer.

The central concern of the narrative is the nature of Nature: if God is present in Nature, does He direct it as a moral force; is it a Satanic agency; or is it an amoral entity acting upon its own volition? Since the natural synecdoche in the story is the destructive sea, the philosophical inquiry resembles that which the orthodox mind of Gerard Manley Hopkins answers with greater resolution in "The Wreck of the Deutschland." Lacking the conviction that Hopkins found in Catholicism, Stevenson creates a symbolic landscape without moral equivalents: Aros Jay as "the house of God," The *Espirito Santo* and the *Christ-Anna,* and the references to St. Columba are each suggestive but lack clear religious significance. Perhaps for this reason the story seems finally unconvincing. Developing his "sonata of the sea and wrecks," Stevenson draws upon the traditional ghost story in order to conclude his narrative events but leaves the ethical questions disturbingly unresolved.

As Stevenson admitted to Henley (Letters, II, 44), "My uncle himself is not the story as I see it, only the leading episode of that story. It's really a story of wrecks, as they appear to the dwellers on the coast. It's a view of the sea." The sea, a primordial given, is somewhat separable from the less constant fictional details. Its interaction with those other details, however, specifically with the Darnaways, constitutes both the literal and symbolic narrative movement. The story is told by Charles Darnaway, who by his language and action represents the somewhat confused ethical norm.

A visitor to Aros on previous vacations from Edinburgh University, Charles now arrives there with two specific intentions: to marry his cousin Mary (and thus unite his dying family), and to hunt for buried Spanish gold so that he may restore his family "to its longforgotten dignity and wealth." His impulse toward family restoration is commendable, but his method of restoration is nothing less than plunder, the same kind of plunder for which he later upbraids his uncle. Charles is more cautious than his uncle about stealing; not so convinced in his defiance of nature; and, when in his search he comes upon the fragmentary remains of a dead man, he takes this discovery as a sign that he should "meddle no more with the spoils of wrecked vessels or the treasures of the dead." Having saved himself from desecration, he becomes his uncle's moral goad. Charles, however, possesses neither greater goodness nor wisdom than his uncle, merely a sense of balance which Gordon's enforced isolation has destroyed. Thus his admonitions prove appropriately futile, and he succeeds only in unwittingly blocking his uncle's last means of escape.

Gordon Darnaway, another of those magnificent cowards so prominent in Stevenson's fiction, towers over the other characters somewhat disproportionately; he is equaled only by The Merry Men, the breakers whose power he covets. A refugee from life's ill-fortune, he has retired to the islet of Aros so that he may "bite his nails at destiny"; and he lives there in constant fear of the sea whose spoils he shares. His fear is conditioned by an intense self-awareness and by a profound sense of guilt fanned by his Cameronian conscience. A man of outward piety, he is inwardly a creature of intense instability, subject to the slightest reminder of his actions. Two of these reminders are ever present: a shadowlike substance which he believes to be a sea creature come to take its revenge, and the grave of a supposed murder victim whose life was seemingly forfeited to his greed. Gordon, plagued by inescapable guilt, seeks solace in the destructive force of the sea in which he sees a contrast to his own cowardice. Lying upon the cove looking out upon a foundering ship in the throes of The Merry Men, he glories in the combat from which he has retired; but he savors the stores which the waves will throw up to ease his discomfort. A voyeur of greater dimensions than either Silas or Mr. Malthus, he vicariously defies the God whom he believes to be immanent in the sea's wreckage. Only when a black man emerges from one of the wrecks does Gordon's fear of a pursuing demon overcome his defiance, and he runs from this graphic reminder of his sinfulness until both plunge into the "redeeming" waters.

The excitement of the final chase diguises its ethical uncertainty. Gordon's death is more satisfying as a conclusion than as an answer to the philosophical questions his actions raise. The black man, although a striking figure, is too patently a device to carry the weight of his literal and symbolic values. Characteristic ambiguity here seems more like equivocation, as if Stevenson hoped that a whirl of adventure would compensate for a lack of depth. In his best fiction—*Jekyll and Hyde, Treasure Island, Kidnapped, Weir of Hermiston*—romance is a legitimate world view; but in this story it is a retreat, a withdrawal by a reluctant realist from the conclusions which realism threatens: "but with all my romance, I am a realist and a prosaist, and a most fanatical lover of plain physical sensation plainly and expressly rendered; hence my perils" (Letters, IV, 48).

Stevenson is reluctant to pursue the implications of Gordon's actions, for to do so is to admit a truth from which he purposely shied away: to see sinful man in the hands of an angry God, or an angry universe, with no release but death. Unwilling to admit such a grim conclusion, he is also unable to offer an alternative. The disappointingly artificial ending serves to emphasize Stevenson's intellectual hesitation. More than the other stories in the collection, "The Merry Men" represents an advance in fictional technique, but like them it remains strikingly incomplete.

III   Island Nights' Entertainments

Stevenson's South Seas stories, like his poems and essays, say more about his own sense of exile than about their location. Beset by personal difficulties, he struggled to make his existence meaningful while away from a civilization whose values he never abandoned.[12] His fiction is a correlative of his personal predicament; and his characters, people like himself, are unable either to return to their homeland or to accommodate themselves to their present situation. More than he, however, they are white men lost in a tropical paradise which for them is hell. In a grim transformation which underscores Stevenson's final disillusionment, "the golden apples" which grow "below another sky" have turned to ash.

Of the three stories in *Island Nights' Entertainments* (perhaps an intended echo of *Arabian Nights' Entertainments*), the most successful is "The Beach of Falesà." "The Bottle Imp" and "The Isle of Voices" are conventional narratives whose settings are more a matter of convenience than a necessity. The first is still another variant of the treasure hunt motif and is acknowledgedly derived from a popular stage melodrama, while the second is like a prose ballad weighted down with that native superstition which the realism of "The Beach of Falesà" transcends. It is this transcendence of simple belief and its obvious representation—"no supernatural trick at all"—that Stevenson refers to in his consideration of "The Beach of Falesà" as "the first realistic South Sea story" (Letters, III, 292). His intention was to present life in the South Seas as it really was for the European with nowhere else to go.

Stevenson considered the crucial item in "The Beach of Falesà" to be John Wiltshire and his first-person narration. He knew that he must allow Plain John Wiltshire (as he called him in an unpublished political tract) [13] to set both the narrative and the moral tone. In his success, he created one of his most intriguing characters: bluff, chauvinistic, outspoken, simple, and kind, Wiltshire personifies both the best and worst of his countrymen—John Bull "gone native." An unsuccessful trader, he arrives on the island of Falesà from a lonely outpost, eager for money and white companionship. Never fond of the "Kanakas," he brings to his new post a dislike intensified by isolation from his countrymen. Yet the white men he meets prove to be the cause of Falesà's ills; and he finds, much to his surprise, that it is he who must cleanse the island of their corruption and then settle down with a native wife and a family of half-castes.

All of this happens to Wiltshire despite his original intentions, for his initial desire is to earn enough money so that he may return to England to run a pub. He is at first quite willing to follow the lead of the dishonest whites, especially the enviable Case. What saves Wiltshire, however, is his honesty, a frankness, brutal at times, which would no sooner cheat than be cheated. In place of the whites, he turns to Uma, his native wife, who returns his love and compassion with an affection not customary in the hasty "marriages" common in the islands. With her help, he succeeds in killing Case and ridding the island of his influence. Wiltshire's story is purposely marked by a series of ironic turns, for his ability to accept irony allows him to persevere: admiring the white men, he exposes their villainy; despising the natives, he becomes their savior; hoping to gain enough money to leave the islands forever, he commits himself to a family loyalty which insures that he can never go home.

For once, Stevenson's irony is neither grim nor crude; his comedy, neither farce nor parody. Wiltshire's dilemma is of his own making and results from an essential goodness which he could no sooner rid himself of than his own identity. What is more, he knows this; but he has no intention of retreating from whatever comes his way. Challenged by circumstance, he asserts his independence with a characteristically patriotic bluster. While successful beyond most Stevenson protagonists, he still must relinquish his home and his ambition to an enforced exile among people he can never call his own. John Wiltshire is, for the most part, the ideal Stevenson man: forced into a situation contrary to his desires, he "co-endures with his existence" by affirming his willingness to continue; threatened by hostile forces, he never abandons himself either to self-denial or to denial of others.

In contrast to Wiltshire, Case is secretive and withdrawn. He is also surprisingly common, a rather matter-of-fact malefactor whose villainy is dependent upon his ability to manipulate basic human fears. A petty capitalist fanatically determined to maintain his monopoly over Falesà's copra trade, he works upon native superstition in order to frighten competitors. Successful until Wiltshire's arrival, his exposure is fatal both to himself and to the legendary evil which he fabricates. As Case's devils are proved to be mere stage props—eerie lights, banjo strings vibrating in the wind, grotesque masks daubed in luminous paint—evil is seen to be more than what is outwardly discernible or customarily imagined. Rather than being provocatively alluring, it is revealed as unattractively commonplace.

While a small-time entrepreneur, Case is also a representative of a civilized Europe forced into corruption in order to maintain its dominance. It is possible to see in him an example of colonialism's defects which Stevenson closely observed in his travels. Proud of being European, he was nonetheless convinced that the major powers were responsible for creating unnecessary difficulties among the islanders. Case shares with the worst of the colonialists a willingness to deny the best of his own culture while trifling with another. A deflated Colonel Blimp, his actions are a caricature of the colonial mentality: Cecil Rhodes in striped pajamas and straw hat.

Although David Daiches' comparison in *White Man in the Tropics* of "The Beach of Falesà" with Joseph Conrad's "Hearts of Darkness" suggests thematic similarity, the comparison says more about what is not in Stevenson's story than what is. The horror of Conrad's story centers around Kurtz's total submission

A Single Glimpse, A Few Sharp Sounds

to the lure of barbarism which he finds in the jungle and in himself. As Marlowe suggests, to look into the abyss is to peer into the self and see mirrored there the mysterious darkness of the universe. Civilization and barbarism are separated only by the umbilical waters of the Thames and the Congo, and European man is frightfully close to his jungle neighbor. Case, unlike Kurtz, is hardly affected by the horror (neither is Wiltshire); he is more like Conrad's young-man-on-the-make, the would-be assistant manager whom Marlowe appropriately calls a "papier-mâché Mephistopheles." Seeking only personal opportunity, he is concerned· with the native society only as it may benefit him.

Stevenson's concern is likewise not with native society but with a debasement of European civilization—a civilization which for all its faults is still preferable to "a Cycle of Cathay." Case acts contrary to the teachings of that civilization, but Wiltshire upholds its central principles. Like their author, both think of the natives as "barbarous children"; for Case, they are to be exploited; for Wiltshire, they are to be protected. Taken together, both characterize the ambivalent European attitude toward the seemingly inferior native which Stevenson believed in more than he wished to admit. His own behavior in Samoa resembles his praise of a Catholic missionary: "It was part of his policy to live among the natives like an elder brother; to follow where he could; to lead where it was necessary; never to drive; and to encourage the growth of new habits, instead of violently rooting up the old" (*In The South Seas*, XX, 79). There is in this statement an inescapable recollection of Pope Gregory's advice to St. Augustine as he went out to convert the Anglo-Saxons. It clarifies Stevenson's personal and fictional inability to view the South Seas as anything more than a parallel of Europe.

CHAPTER 6

The Anatomy of Dr. Jekyll and Mr. Hyde

NO work of Stevenson's has been so popular or so harmed by its popularity as *The Strange Case of Dr. Jekyll and Mr. Hyde* (1886). As pulpit oratory, as a starring vehicle on stage and screen, as a colloquial metaphor for the good-evil antithesis that lurks in all men, it has become the victim of its own success, allowing subsequent generations to take the translation for the original, to see Jekyll or Hyde where one should see Jekyll-Hyde. A photograph of Richard Mansfield as he played the dual role in T. R. Sullivan's play illustrates the conventional attitude: Jekyll appears as the epitome of goodness—eyes upraised to heaven and one arm lifted in allegiance to heaven's direction—and lacks only a halo to complete his beatitude; Hyde crouches menacingly—hairy, grimacing, unkempt—eager to pounce from within his Jekyllian confines and spread the foul juices of his subversive glands.[1]

While such a view is clearly oversimplified, it is annoyingly persistent (much as the mispronunciation of Jekyll's name).[2] Only a careful reading of the story reveals its formal complexity and its moral depth. As a narrative, it is the most intricately structured of Stevenson's stories; as a fable, it represents a classic touchstone of Victorian sensibilities. It is clearly difficult today to detail each of the responsive chords which the story struck in the Victorian mind, but its use of duality as both a structural and thematic device suggests that its application goes beyond a simple antithesis of moral opposites or physical components. Present evidence indicates that Victorian man was haunted constantly by an inescapable sense of division.[3] As rational and sensual being, as public and private man, as civilized and bestial creature, he found himself necessarily an actor, playing only that part of himself suitable to the occasion. As both variables grew more predictable, his role became more stylized; and what was initially an occasional practice became a way of life. By 1886, the English could already be described as "Masqueraders" (as Henry Arthur Jones portrayed them eight years later), and it is to all aspects of this existential charade that Jekyll and Hyde addresses itself. With characteristic haste, it plunges immediately into the center of Victorian society to dredge up a creature ever present but submerged; not the evil opponent of a contentious good but the shadow self of a half man.

I *The Victorian World*

Because the morality of *Dr. Jekyll and Mr. Hyde* lies at the center of the Victorian world, no detail in the story is so vital as its location. Critics, especially G. K. Chesterton,[4] have been quick to indicate that the morality is actually more Scottish than English and that the more proper setting for the narrative would have been Edinburgh. Yet although Chesterton and others are right in thinking that Stevenson could no more put aside his Scottish heritage here than he could in other stories, they fail to recognize that only London could serve as the *locus classicus* of Victorian behavior. An enigma composed of multiple layers of being, its confines held virtually all classes of society conducting what were essentially independent lives.

In the 1880's, London society could not have been much different from Michael Sadleir's description of it some twenty years before in *Forlorn Sunset* (1947): "London in the early 'sixties was still three parts jungle. Except for the residential and shopping areas . . . hardly a district was really 'public' in the sense that ordinary folk went to and fro. . . . There was no knowing what kind of a queer patch you might strike, in what blind alley you might find yourself, to what embarrassment, insult, or even molestation you might be exposed. So the conventional middle-class kept to the big thoroughfares, conscious that just behind the house-fronts to either side murmured a million hidden lives, but incurious as to their kind, and hardly aware that those who lived there were also London citizens" (21). London was much like its inhabitants, a macrocosm of the necessary fragmentation that Victorian man found inescapable. Unlike Edinburgh with its stark division of Old Town and New, London represented that division-within-essential-unity which is the very meaning of *Jekyll and Hyde*. As both geographic and symbolic center, London exemplified what Stevenson called it in *New Arabian Nights,* "the great battlefield of mankind."

The appropriateness of the London setting may also be seen from a revealing Victorian document, Reverend William Tuckniss's introduction to the fourth volume of Mayhew's *London Labour and the London Poor* (1862) [1968]. Intended as a guide to the several reformative agencies at work to ameliorate the lot of the poor, Tuckniss's introduction has much to say about the city in which those poor eke out their lives. In many ways a moral Baedeker, Tuckniss describes a London teeming with vice while concurrently responsive to religious persuasion. Indeed, he rises to such rhapsody about its mixed nature that one cannot help seeing this mixture as a necessary ingredient for moral reformer and artistic creator alike. "It is in the crowded city, however, that the seeds of good and evil are brought to the highest state of maturity, and virtue and vice most rapidly developed, under the forcing influences that everywhere abound. . . . London then may be considered as the grand central focus of operations, at once the emporium of crime and the palladium of Christianity. It is, in fact, the great arena of conflict between the powers of darkness and the ministry of heaven. . . . It is here that they join issue in the most deadly proximity, and struggle for the vantage-ground" (xiv, xv). Tuckniss's descriptive language is strikingly similar to Stevenson's: in both, London is the essential metaphor, and as "the great battlefield of mankind" or "the great arena of [moral] conflict," it is the vital center of the Victorian world.

Of equal importance to a consideration of *Jekyll and Hyde* are the people who inhabit that world and the manner in which they are presented. Critics have often complained that the London of the story is singularly devoid of women; Stephen Gwynn, for example, likens the atmosphere to "a community of monks" (130) in *Robert Louis Stevenson* (1939). For once it is easy to account for this omission without reference to the bogeyman of Victorian prudery. For better or worse, Victoria's era, despite its monarch, was male-centered; and a story so directed at the essence of its moral behavior is best seen from a male perspective. In addition, and here is where Gwynn's figure is so apt, an air of fierce austerity pervades the story—a peculiarly masculine breed of asceticism which, like the London fog, colors the entire surface. It is as if the atmospheric color were itself a symbol of normative rigidity. The men of the story are representative Victorian types, exemplars of a harsh life that is best seen in the somber context of their professional and social conduct.

The four prominent men in the story are gentlemen and, as such, are variations of standard gentlemanly behavior. Three are professional men—two doctors, one lawyer—and the only nonprofessional, Richard Enfield, is so locked into his role that his description as "the well-known man about town" might as well be a professional designation. The first to be introduced, "Mr. Utterson the lawyer," is characterized immediately by his profession as well as by a somewhat bitter-sweet compound of surface harshness and internal sympathy. Prone to self-mortification in order to stifle temptation, he nonetheless confines his rigorous standard to himself. With others, he is not only tolerant but charitable, as he translates compassion into action. Feigning unconcern, he often remains "the last good influence in the lives of down-going men." Clearly the moral norm of the story, Utterson is introduced first not only because he is Jekyll's confidant (the only one remaining) but because by person and profession he represents the best and worst of Victoria's social beings. Pledged to a code harsh in its application, he has not allowed its pressures to mar his sense of human need. For himself, he has chosen; and he must make his life on that choice; but he judges others with the understanding necessary to human weakness.

As a lawyer, he represents that legality which identifies social behavior as established law, unwritten but binding; as a judge, however, he is a combination of justice and mercy (as his names Gabriel John suggest), tempering rigidity with kindness, self-denial with compassion. His reaction to Hyde must be seen in this context. While Hyde's grim visage seems sufficient to alarm even the most objective observer (witness the Edinburgh apothecary), Hyde's threat to Jekyll's reputation, and possibly his person, makes him even more frightening to Utterson, a partisan in the best sense of the term, and loyal to his friends especially in their adversity. Utterson is the essence of what Stevenson meant in "Reflections and Remarks on Human Life" when he said: "It is the business of this life to make excuses for others. . . . Even justice is no right of a man's own, but a thing . . . which he should strive to see rendered to another" (South Seas edition, XIV, 213).

Utterson's walking companion, and the narrator of Hyde's first "crime," Richard Enfield, appears as a strange, yet appropriate, complement to his distant kinsman. Described as "a well-known man about town," his haunts and habits ("I was coming home from some place at the end of the world, about three o'clock of a black winter morning") seem the "other Victorian" side of Utterson's sobriety. Yet even their casual friendship suggests a combination evidently not impossible in the Victorian social world. Their dull but necessary weekly stroll represents a public acknowledgement of a possibility that Henry Jekyll, for one, was unwilling to admit; and it reinforces the belief that the "other Victorians" are very much the Victorians one has always known but only recently grown to understand. As distant as Utterson appears to be, Enfield is the model of detached experience inured to much of life's ugliness (Utterson calls him "unimpressionable"). Thus, when he describes Hyde as "displeasing" and "detestable," his verdict may be seen as more objective and more knowledgeable than his kinsman's.

While Utterson and Enfield complement each other's limitations, Lanyon and Jekyll reveal each other's emptiness. Eminent medical men with an initial "bond of common interest," they have severed their bond over what seems a professional quarrel— Jekyll's metaphysical speculations about human identity which Lanyon admits were "too fanciful." Lanyon, however, has made not so much a professional judgement as a personal one; he has refrained from following Jekyll because of cowardice rather than because of conviction. If Jekyll's inquiries were "too fanciful," they were so because Lanyon lacked the courage, though not the curiosity, to follow him; and his horror at the discovery that Hyde and Jekyll are actually one is as much a self-realization as it is a condemnation of his former friend. Lanyon abandoned Jekyll because he was afraid of the temptation to which he finally succumbed, the offer made so perfectly by the serpentine Hyde coaxing the more-than-willing Lanyon to discover "a new province of knowledge and new avenues to fame and power." A friend in name only, his envy of Jekyll works in direct contrast to that which prompts Utterson to loyalty. Like Jekyll, Lanyon's outward manner belies his inner compulsions; but, unlike his colleague, he cannot struggle with their emergence.

Henry Jekyll, however, is nobody's hero. Although his actions are prompted by no single motive, his primary impulse is fear. If Lanyon is afraid to admit vital truths about himself, Jekyll fears these same truths when he discovers them. Dedicated to an ethical rigidity more severe than Utterson's, because solely self-centered, he cannot face the necessary containment of his dual being. However he may attempt to disguise his experiments under scientific objectivity, and his actions under a macabre alter-ego, he is unable to mask his basic selfishness. As he reveals in his final statement (the bare legal term is better than the more sentimental "confession"), he has thrived upon duplicity; and his reputation has been maintained largely upon his successful ability to deceive. Yet he is no ordinary hypocrite, a simple analogue of such other Stevenson characters as Deacon Brodie. Although Jekyll is unable to judge himself accurately, he is right in denying his hypocrisy. Only briefly does he pretend to be someone other than himself. Having recognized his duality, he attempts to isolate his two selves into individual beings and to allow each to go his separate way. Mere disguise is never sufficient for his ambition; and his failure goes beyond hypocrisy, a violation of social honesty, until it touches upon moral transgression, a violation of the physical and metaphysical foundations of human existence. Henry Jekyll is a complex example of his age of anxiety: woefully weighed down by self-deception, cruelly a slave to his own weakness, sadly a disciple of a severe discipline, his is a voice out of "De Profundis," a cry of Victorian man from the depths of his self-imposed underground.

Henry Jekyll's fiction is to identify that underground man as Edward Hyde. The fiction of the story, however, confirms the insoluble duality of his being. Each of the successive narratives strengthens that inherent union of antagonistic forces which Jekyll attempts to deny. In each, the reader learns more about both Jekyll and Hyde. Unlike conventional narratives in which the action usually develops with a continuous depiction of incident, the matter of *Jekyll and Hyde* ends only after the several incidents have been illuminated by subjective comment. For example, the cold objective horror of the maid's description as Hyde pounces upon the unsuspecting Sir Danvers Carew is balanced by the tormented narratives of a pitiful Lanyon and a compulsive Jekyll. The measure of this story is thus not only in its characters' actions but in their narrations of those actions. Nothing in the story is as singly frightening as Henry Jekyll's final narrative, for in it the reader learns most about the distorted mind which released an unwilling Hyde.

II *The Narrative Voices*

The three separable narrative voices—Enfield, Lanyon, Jekyll—are placed in successive order so that they add increasing rhetorical and psychological dimension to the events they describe. In contrast to other multiple narratives whose several perspectives often raise questions of subjective truth and moral ambiguity, these individual narratives in *Jekyll and Hyde* provide a linear regularity of information—an incremental catalogue of attitudes toward Hyde's repulsiveness and Jekyll's decline.[5] Enfield's narrative is the briefest since it describes Hyde's trampling a little girl; and the salient items in it are Enfield's unsuccessful attempts at objectivity and the horrified reactions of the other spectators. To Enfield, it is not the collision itself which is of primary importance but Hyde's casual indifference to the screaming agonies of his victim. Hyde violates a norm of respectable behavior, and his subsequent offer of monetary retribution is nothing more than automatic. Enfield's description, therefore, accentuates Hyde's mechanical regularity in contrast to the human concern which a gentleman should display (does Enfield recognize the artificiality of convention?). Thus, objective as he would be by first describing Hyde as a little man with a stumping gait, his rising gorge forces his language toward the metaphors of "hellish," "damned Juggernaut," and "Satan."

Enfield, however, is reacting to an action which he had personally witnessed. More surprising is the reaction of the hate-filled crowd that gathers around the cornered Hyde, for the people respond not to the trampling but to Hyde's physical repulsiveness. Of these, none is more representative than the doctor who comes to attend the child. A cut-and-dry Edinburgh apothecary, the most general of general practitioners, "about as emotional as a bagpipe," he cannot mask a fierce desire to kill Hyde even as he looks at him. The first of the story's three doctors, he represents what might be regarded as the normative medical mind. Placed here as an effective contrast to his more ambitious colleagues Lanyon and Jekyll, the apothecary's immediate, physical loathing foreshadows the later revelation that Hyde is more than a stunted figure of a man, that he is in truth an amoral abstraction.

Lanyon's and Jekyll's narratives follow immediatley upon each other, and both are voices from the grave. As Enfield's narrative is meant as an introduction to the dual existence of Jekyll-Hyde, their narratives occur appropriately after that existence has been concluded. Before either may comment, it is necessary that Hyde emerge with uncontrollable suddenness and commit a murder from which there is no escape but death. By the time of Lanyon's narrative, the reader knows that the Hyde whose misdeeds he has been following has killed himself; but he only suspects that Henry Jekyll has also died. Lanyon's narrative is the first to reveal the truth about the Jekyll-Hyde relationship at the same time that it confirms the grim dominance of Hyde and his magnetic "glittering eye." The whole substance of his narrative is meant to carry Hyde beyond the automatic and rather innocent actions of the Enfield narrative so that he may now be seen as truly diabolical. If Enfield's Hyde was a Juggernaut, Lanyon's is a cunning tempter ruthlessly proud of his ability.

Only after the reader has experienced the revelation of Lanyon's narrative does Stevenson permit him Jekyll's "Full Statement," one which should be read not simply as an appropriate conclusion to the narrative action but as the culmination of the multiple-narrative technique. More than the other narratives, it attempts to present some insight into the narrator's psychology at the same time that it chronicles the process of his destruction. It thus proceeds in two complementary directions: a progressive exposition of events verifiable by their previous occurrence, and an explanation of those events necessarily ambiguous since they are offered by a man incapable of self-judgment. Indeed, the structure of Jekyll's statement is directed toward an often inadvertent self-revelation which proves conclusively that his selfishness and moral cowardice released the horrible personification of his hidden drives. This is not to say that Jekyll is a fiend; he is one no more so than Hyde. Yet, with increasing evidence, he incriminates himself as the guilty party in an indivisible relationship.

Jekyll also details the legitimate scientific concerns which prompted his experiment. His error, however, is that he used these as excuses; but the reader can view them only as explanations. Because of his self-delusion, Jekyll remains unaware of the true results of his experiment; until the end, he believes that Hyde "concerns another than myself." Never able to see beyond his initial deception, he learns little about himself or about the essential failure of his experiment, and remains convinced that the incompatible parts of his being can be separated if the pure powder were available. This conviction, as much as anything else, is Henry Jekyll's tragedy. He is so enmeshed in his self-woven net of duplicity that he cannot identify the two entities whose separation he hopes to achieve. By seeing Hyde as another being rather than as part of himself, he is forced to deny the most significant result of his experiment and indeed of his entire story: the inescapable conclusion that man must dwell in uncomfortable but necessary harmony with his multiple selves. The final suicide is thus fittingly a dual effort: though the hand that administers the poison is Edward Hyde's, Henry Jekyll forces the action. Never before have they been so much one as when Hyde insures the realization of Jekyll's death-wish.

III *The Symbolic Structure*

Stevenson's fictional abilities are further evidenced by his successful insertion of thematic contrasts into the narrative structure itself. The topography of *Jekyll and Hyde* may be seen as a study in symbolic location, a carefully worked out series of contrasts between exterior modes and interior realities. Like much of Victorian life and letters, most of the story's action is physically internalized behind four walls.[6] Utterson's ruminations, Lanyon's seduction, and Jekyll-Hyde's death all occur within the protective confines of what Stevenson in an essay termed "The Ideal House." Although, as Walter Houghton has observed,[7] the Victorian home was often a temple of domestic virtues, it also served as a shelter —a screen not only from the threatening forces of the new age but from the all-seeing eye of Mrs. Grundy. In an age of increasing privatization, it could not be otherwise.[8]

While the structure of *Jekyll and Hyde* is predicated upon a contrast between exterior and interior, the contrast is never allowed to remain static. The actions that occur in each represent an intriguing paradox: in the exterior, social ambles and foul crimes; in the interior, elegant drawing rooms and secreted laboratories. Each division contains two opposing elements which combine to characterize the individual locale, but both locations in their necessary union represent the social cosmos. The result is a social bond no less indivisible than the moral bond which Jekyll attempts unsuccessfully to sever. The central metaphor is Jekyll's house, with its sinister rear entrance through which Hyde passes and its handsome front "which wore a great air of wealth and comfort": the two faces of Jekyll contained in one inseparable dwelling.

The paradox is continued as the action of *Jekyll and Hyde* becomes internalized. The two final subjective accounts solidify this process on a psychological level, and the action itself leads farther and farther into the interior of Jekyll's house. Although the reader's first views of the house are external, the action soon directs him to the hall, then to the study, and finally to the ominous experiments behind the closed door of the former dissection laboratory. As Poole and Utterson break down the last barrier to Jekyll's secret, they literally and metaphorically destroy his one remaining refuge; by invading his physical sanctuary, they force him into a psychological admission whose only possibility is death. Stevenson's skillful juggling of literal and metaphoric—his ability to suggest the symbolic significance of commonplace reality—is undoubtedly the chief difference between the original bogey story to which his wife, Fanny, objected and the classic fable which *Jekyll and Hyde* has become.[9] Clearly, the most telling evidence of this skill is his ability to select highly suggestive scenery and to allow its multiple suggestions to form the several layers of his narrative.

IV Hyde As Metaphor

For reader and nonreader alike, the crucial item of thematic significance has been Edward Hyde. Unquestionably the dominant character, his role in the narrative is often considered the fictional mechanism by which the moral truths are driven home. Surely such a reading is partial, for it fails to approach the story as a total construct and thus commits the sin of facile separation only a trifle less grievous than Jekyll's. Yet Hyde's identity, both physical and moral, is the pervasive mystery whose elusiveness and final revelation unites the fictional and moral concerns. Without Jekyll, there could never have been a Hyde; without Hyde, one can never fully know Jekyll. Thus an ability to understand their relationship rests on an ability to identify what Hyde represents. To begin negatively, he is not the antithetical evil to Jekyll's good nor is he evil at all. His cruelty derives from his association with Jekyll, not from any inherent motivation toward destruction. True, he is compulsive (as is Jekyll), a veritable Juggernaut proceeding on his mechanical way; but this characteristic is primarily found in his initial movements when Jekyll's desires first spring him from his lair. One of the more fascinating developments in the story is Hyde's growing malice—his increasing premeditation as he becomes more and more a mortal.

Furthermore, he is not the physical manifestation of Jekyll's id too long repressed by a leering ego. This sexual reading has contributed perhaps more than any other to the vulgarization of Stevenson's intentions, and as early as 1887 he recognized its threat. Responding to a letter from John Paul Bocock, then editor of the *New York Sun,* he attempted to counter Richard Mansfield's distortions: "You are right as to Mansfield: Hyde was the younger of the two. He was not . . . Great Gods! a mere voluptuary. There is no harm in a voluptuary; and none, with my hand on my heart and in the sight of God, none—no harm whatever in what prurient fools call 'immorality.' The harm was in Jekyll, because he was a hypocrite—not because he was fond of women; he says so himself, but people are so filled full of folly and inverted lust, that they can think of nothing but sexuality." [10]

Stevenson's letter is a necessary antidote to a spreading malignancy, but its effect has been relatively nugatory. The legendary Hyde is obviously a difficult opponent. There is clearly something consolatory about equating Hyde with illicit sex; it localizes one's impulses and allows indulgences within the proprieties. Stevenson's Hyde, on the other hand, though less formidable, is more substantial. His substantiality increases, in fact, in direct proportion to his recognition as the essence of man's natural vitality. The key word is *natural,* for it governs the entire amoral world from which Hyde emerges. As the mirror of Jekyll's inner compulsions, he represents that shadow side of man which civilization has striven to submerge: he is a creature of primitive sensibilities loosed upon a world bent on denying him. A reminder of the barbarism which underlies civilization, he is a necessary component of human psychology which most would prefer to leave unrealized.

As an essential life force, Hyde's proper role is to act in harmony with the other parts of man's being. The ideal is expressed in Stevenson's essay, "Lay Morals": "[The soul] demands that we should not live alternately with our opposing tendencies in continual see-saw of passion and disgust, but seek some path on which the tendencies shall no longer oppose, but serve each other to common end. . . . The soul demands unity of purpose, not the dismemberment of man; it seeks to roll up all his strength and sweetness, all his passion and wisdom, into one, and make of him a perfect man exulting in perfection" (II, 179). Yet Stevenson, like Arnold before him, recognized that the ideal of "*one* aim, *one* business, *one* desire" is an El Dorado of the soul's pursuit.

Throughout his writings Stevenson dwells upon the inescapable burden which any relationship between the barbaric and the civilized produces. Painfully aware of the difficulties their conjunction necessitates, he continues to affirm their vital correspondence. In his essays, the expression is often a cosmic groan—"For nowadays the pride of man denies in vain his kinship with the original dust. . . . The whole creation groaneth and travaileth together" ("Pulvis et Umbra," XIII, 205); in his letters, an involuntary gasp—"*Jekyll* is a dreadful thing I own; but the only thing I feel dreadful about is that damned old business of the war in the members. This time it came out; I hope it will stay in, in the future" (Letter to John Addington Symonds, II, 292); in the fiction, an unavoidable admission—"I have been made to learn that the doom and burthen of our life is bound for ever on man's shoulders, and when the attempt is made to cast it off, it but returns upon us with more unfamiliar and more awful pressure" (*Jekyll and Hyde*, X, 71).

Although the last statement is Jekyll's, the sentiments are Stevenson's; they could have been spoken by several of his fictional characters who are much like Jekyll—Markheim, Brodie, Herrick, Henry Durie—for they indicate an essential conclusion toward which much of the fiction is directed. In his fiction in particular Stevenson develops this double strain of being; there he illustrates the inevitable conflict between natural urges and societal pressures, and there he presents the tragedy of those who surrender themselves to either.

Jekyll surrenders to his society. "The harm [that] was in Jekyll" was in large part the harm of Victoria's England; and his unwillingness to acknowledge his kinship with Edward Hyde may be likened to everyone else's intense hatred of his moral twin. The universal hatred directed at Hyde both in and out of the story is a striking verification of the extent to which Victorian England feared what he represented. Jekyll's repugnance is scarcely his alone, and his actions are predicated upon a social ethic only slightly less distorted than his moral myopia. Victorian anxieties contributed greatly to *Jekyll and Hyde's* success. The fictional paradox revealed the social paradox; Jekyll's dilemma spoke for more of his countrymen than many were willing to admit.

If Jekyll's fears are taken as a barometer of Victorian anxieties, his relationship to Hyde becomes apparent. While Jekyll represents a man "in the pink of the proprieties," Hyde is the brutal embodiment of the moral, social, political, and economic threats which shook the uncertain Victorian world. In his moral role, he exemplifies the impossibility of any successful separation of man's natural being. A metaphysical impulse in a postlapsarian world, any attempted return to Eden (he proves) must be made at the cost of one's life. Likewise, his social identity cautions the attempted imposition of a new Manicheanism based upon a dichotomy between external and internal behavior. As G. K. Chesterton recognized in *Robert Louis Stevenson,* "The real stab of the story is not in the discovery that the one man is two men; but in the discovery that the two men are one man. . . . The point of the story is not that a man *can* cut himself off from his conscience, but that he cannot" (72).

As political and economic man, Hyde's role is more subtle. The inevitability of his brute power, his unceasing energy, no doubt recalled to many the threatening forces which were beating upon the solid doors of their comfortable homes. Hidden in them as he was, Victorian man could not for long confine himself beneath the domestic covers.[11] He feared "the armies of the night," the troops of the new politics and the new economics that were massing for the onslaught. Two examples clarify this context: the first is Dickens' Wemmick in *Great Expectations,* who, beset by the requisites of the new economics, finds it necessary to become a double man, a public and a private personality. His fortresslike house is a singularly apt metaphor for the fearful manner in which Victorian man attempted to withdraw behind his solid wall of comfort. Wemmick is a comic variant of Jekyll-Hyde, for he finds a solution which, if limited, is nonetheless salutary. The second example is a comment from H. V. Routh's *Money, Morals, and Manners as Revealed in Modern Literature* (1935): "the typical upper class Victorian was haunted by a ghost, a dry-featured dwarfish caricature of himself unpleasantly like the *economic man*" (141). Few descriptions of Hyde have been better.

Stevenson's story contains no description more precise. Hyde is usually described in metaphors because essentially that is what he is: a metaphor of uncontrolled appetites, an amoral abstraction driven by a compelling will unrestrained by any moral halter. Such a creature is, of necessity, only figuratively describable; for his deformity is moral rather than physical. Purposely left vague, he is best described as Jekyll-deformed—dwarfish, stumping, ape-like—a frightening parody of a man unable to exist on the surface. He and Jekyll are inextricably joined because one without the other cannot function in society. As Hyde is Jekyll's initial disguise, so Jekyll is Hyde's refuge after the Carew murder. If Jekyll reflects respectability, then Hyde is his image "through the looking glass."

Hyde's literal power ends with his suicide, but his metaphorical power is seemingly infinite. Many things to his contemporaries, he has grown beyond Stevenson's story in an age of automatic Freudian response.[12] As Hyde has grown, Jekyll has been overshadowed so that his role has shifted from culprit to victim. Accordingly, the original fable has assumed a meaning neither significant for the nineteenth century nor substantial for the twentieth. The time has come for Jekyll and Hyde to be put back together again.

CHAPTER 7

A Pursuit of Nightingales

E ACH of Stevenson's novels attempts to illustrate the possibility of romance in the modern world. From *Treasure Island*
(1883) to *Weir of Hermiston* (1894) they exhibit similar conflicts
and irresolutions. Written wherever Stevenson found temporary
comfort, they range in location from Scotland to the South Seas,
and in structure from boy's adventure to a balladlike reminiscence. All have marked similarities, yet each has its particular
identity, its own unique experience.

Criticism of the novels has usually maintained two constants:
that Stevenson's narratives are essentially romances, and that
their quality improves as they discard the barbarisms of their
romance antecedents and strive toward a greater realism. As
Frank Swinnerton wrote in *Robert Louis Stevenson: A Critical
Study* (1923), "Therefore when I say that Stevenson progressed as a novelist and as a tale-teller from romance to realism
I hope to be absolved of any wish to suit facts to a theory. The
fact that he so progressed simply is there, and that should be
sufficient" (133). Similarly, Edwin Eigner asserted in 1966, in
Robert Louis Stevenson and Romance Tradition, that ". . . while
Stevenson participated at times in the Scott and M. G. Lewis tradition of romance, he did not, like Bulwer, confuse this sort of
diablerie with ideas belonging to the more serious romance
tradition" (34). Although more aware of Stevenson's intentions,
Eigner implies what Swinnerton declares with such casual dog-
matism. His suggestion (following Leavis) of a Jekyll-and-Hyde
romance tradition ignores the inseparability of what is essentially
a single view of experience.

The difficulty with such assertions is that, like most distortions,
they contain some truth. Stevenson is very much a romancer,
and it is impossible to understand his fiction without understanding his meaning of that term. Likewise, *Weir of Hermiston* re-

veals a dimension only hinted at previously, but its success represents an extension of adventure fiction, a synthesis of narrative detail which looks toward that ideal Stevenson considered the highest point of all literature: "In the highest achievement of the art of words, the dramatic and the pictorial, the moral and romantic interest rise and fall together by a common and organic law. Situation is animated with passion, passion clothed upon with situation. Neither exists for itself, but each adheres indissolubly with the other" ("A Gossip on Romance," XIII, 139).

Stevensonian romance establishes a chimera of human expectations in which both character and reader are tested by the brute circumstances of their condition. As a verbal daydream merging into pictorial wish fulfillment, it permits both to transcend the commonplace for a world that is always realizable because it is never realized.[1] The narrative movement is toward an assertion of vitality, an attempt to deny the deathlike grip of modern civilization by reaching toward the instinctively recognizable. The essence of this romance lies in its identifiable situations, the incidents which permit the reader to play at being the hero, and, even more, to identify so closely with the action that "we forget the characters, then we push the hero aside; then we plunge into the tale in our own person and bathe in fresh experience, and then, and then only, do we say we have been reading a romance" ("A Gossip on Romance," XIII, 142).

The word "bathe" is particularly appropriate, for romance not only cleanses the cumbersome residue of civilization but allows rebirth into a world of amoral innocence, a baptism that demands total immersion with the promise of spiritual renewal. The romancer's burden is to create such incidents as will enable the reader to transcend the present. Although these will never be exactly the same, they must be filled with necessary suggestion; they must speak clearly to those who would hear "the mermaids singing." The ideal romantic situation forces the reader to plunge immediately into the center of the action to make decisions which he can hardly pause to consider. The greater the action—"the shock of arms or the diplomacy of life"—and the more compelling the circumstance, the more a narrative may be called a romance.

Stevenson's extended narratives are all romances. They contain exciting incidents designed to stimulate the reader—situations sufficiently responsive to his subconscious drives to form a pattern of modern myth. As mythmaker, Stevenson creates narratives which incorporate those situations, incidents, characters, and locations which he believes most significant for his audience. His fictional world is fragmented and severe; it is a world of physical hardship and spiritual isolation in which man is separated from his domestic comfort and from his social and moral authority. His stories are set at land's end amid the bleak coasts of Scotland and England, or on an island apart from the mainland's security.

His protagonists are often children or childlike creatures, barely able to survive in a world in which they are hunted in a nightmare of pursuit and misplaced allegiance. They are thrown upon adventure because they are at odds with the established authority which they have been taught to recognize. As if this were not disjunctive enough, they are often alone. As youths, they are either orphans (David Balfour, Richard Shelton), or separated from their remaining parent (Jim Hawkins, Loudon Dodd), or the emotional nucleus of a disoriented marriage (Archie Weir). As adults, they are estranged from their family (Robert Herrick), or burdened with familial responsibility for which they are unprepared (Henry Durie, St. Ives).

Stevenson's romances are grim reminders of the modern condition in which man finds himself in frightful isolation. Yet he does not place man in this predicament to laugh at his follies or to condemn him to an exitless eternity. His object is to present experience as neutral, a series of events whose function is its own existence, and he promises at least partial achievement to those who actively meet its challenge. In evoking the timeless fears behind modern anxieties, he offers the opportunity to transform those fears into meaningful action. Although action may never be more than reflex—indeed, many of Stevenson's heroes depend upon others to extricate them from their hasty decisions—it is a necessary prelude to adventure.

Adventure is the hope of freedom; it is "the call of the wild" which echoes from beyond the confines of civilization and envisions a journey backward into an unknown future. Stevenson's protagonists are all somewhat like Robert Browning's Childe Roland who, after overcoming the vicissitudes of the eternal wasteland, accepts the challenge of the mysterious unknown. Uncertain of what may be, Roland achieves victory by his arrival at the dark tower. If Stevenson's "heroes" rarely get to signal their victory, they at least accept their "dark towers" with grudging reluctance.

Boyhood adventure is the purest form of Stevensonian romance. It is built upon the fantasies of a childlike imagination, and it is in embryo what will later emerge as suspicion, faithlessness, and ultimate despair. While it remains youthful, however, it retains a freshness of vision which is vital, vibrant, and suggestive of possibility. The four novels of boyhood adventure— *Treasure Island* (1883), *The Black Arrow* (1883), *Kidnapped* (1886), and *Catriona* (1892)—present a world beneath the palimpsest of civilization in which primitive passion, impulsive action, and casual betrayal are a way of life. Within narratives of shocking brutality yet playful innocence, Stevenson recreates a childhood vision of life in which the child is removed from his native isolation and placed among crude experience. The central character in each novel is a youth who, beset by life's "aching joys" and but half-formed, must undergo a journey into experience before achieving even partial self-knowledge. The narrative is a spiritual *bildungsroman* in which the child's physical adventure is translated into moral lesson. At the conclusion of his adventure, although the change may not always be readily apparent, his experiences have lessened his initial provincialism. Having been tested, he stands between childhood promise and adult regret; he is not yet tormented by remorseful nostalgia, but he is no longer secure behind the walled garden.

I Treasure Island

As the narrator of *Treasure Island,* Jim Hawkins is in many ways the prototype of Stevenson's youthful adventurers. He is not only the first, but the least complex; and his story is without many of the intricacies which are found in the subsequent adventures of Richard Shelton in *The Black Arrow* and David Balfour in *Kidnapped.* Although Jim Hawkins's story in *Treasure Island* is not without its structural subtleties and moral ambiguities, Stevenson has him present his adventures in a great rush, with a maximum of excitement and with a minimum of analysis. The object is immediacy of detail to insure immediacy of recognition. Jim is carried upon his voyage by a series of events whose rapidity leave both him and the reader little time for reflection. Both character and reader are captivated by the fascination of treasure, the crude equivalent of the idealized romantic quest, and both board the *Hispaniola* with eager and suspicious anticipation. In Jim, Stevenson creates an archetypal boy—lonely, impressionable, honest, fearful—and constructs a narrative of his adventures whose success depends upon that lightninglike concision which is the hallmark of the Stevenson style.

The first paragraph in *Treasure Island* is a good example of Stevenson's narrative technique; it is also a model of romance suggestion. Its single sentence conveys a marvelous haste as it plunges the reader directly into the action. He learns at once that the story is to be told by one of the participants in an adventure; the adventure is to concern buried treasure, some of which still remains on the island where it was concealed; the adventurers are gentlemen who hope to benefit from their discovery; and their adversaries in the hunt are pirates. Few openings engage the reader so quickly. By the end of the first chapter all the elements of the subsequent action are established and the polarities drawn: Billy Bones has settled at the "Admiral Benbow" and threatened its peaceful isolation; the values of respectability have been challenged by the lure of buried treasure; boyish adventure is about to be turned into mercantile speculation; and the comforts of a lonely cove on the Bristol road are to be exchanged for the damp, feverish swamp of Treasure Island.

The necessary romantic ingredients are presented quickly and sparingly; the manning of the *Hispaniola*, the duplicity of Silver, Jim's accidental discovery of the intended mutiny and his subsequent heroics, the bloody trail to the marked spot only to discover that Ben Gunn had made away with most of the gold, and the final settlement of the money upon those few who survive the adventure. Little wonder Gladstone stayed up all night to read it.[2] Yet the richness of *Treasure Island* goes beyond exciting action and narrative rapidity, essential as these are to its success. Within its narrative directness, it raises questions of social conduct and moral concern which do not usually appear in conventional adventure tales. The real measure of Stevenson's success is his ability to introduce these considerations without upsetting the delicate balance of make-believe. The people of *Treasure Island* are real and unreal; for the most part, they exist in a timeless, spaceless world removed from the incursions of a shattering reality; they are the "puppets" Stevenson intended them to be. On the other hand, they are motivated by all-too-human passions, and they enact a paradigm of that commercial spirit which has become the basis of modern capitalism.

The differences between *Treasure Island* and conventional adventure fiction suggest Stevenson's extension of the form, as David Daiches has indicated in *Stevenson and the Art of Fiction* (1951): "In Stevenson heroic endeavor is not automatically linked to obvious moral goodness; what we admire is not always what we approve of; energy of personality belongs to Long John Silver and not to any conventional hero; and the virtuous are saved in the end almost contemptuously by Lady Luck and an irresponsible boy who does not quite know what he is doing. . . . The characters for whom our sympathies are enlisted go off after hidden treasure out of casual greed, and when their adventure is over have really achieved very little except a modicum of self-knowledge. And Silver, magnificent and evil, disappears into the unknown, the moral ambiguities of his character presented but unexplored" (9).

That few readers have realized these variations is a tribute to Stevenson's ability. As popular as it has become, *Treasure Island* is possibly the strangest adventure story ever written, for it is a boy's book without a hero and without a satisfying conclusion. Furthermore, it recalls for young and old the truths about themselves and their society which they may wish to forget. The young reader cannot shy away from the suggestions of youth's limitations: its nightmarish loneliness; its tangential relationship to the adult society; its impulsive action only sometimes successful, often foolish; and its inability to know others and especially itself. The adult reader faces more painful truths: he must confront the emptiness of that which he has striven to achieve, and he must acknowledge the valid analogy of the treasure hunt with the competitive society from which he draws his values.

From the very beginning the metaphor of money dominates the action: Billy Bones is fearful of discovery because he is privy to the secret of the treasure; Jim's mother is a combination of honesty and greed (as he describes her) as she forages the dead Billy's seaman's chest so that she may take her rightful due; Squire Trelawny dreams of "money to eat—to roll in—to play duck-and-drake with ever after"; and Dr. Livesey commends the death of Pew while rapaciously pocketing the oilskin packet whose contents spell unearned riches. As if this delineation were not sufficient, there is Long John Silver, whose surname embellishes the narrative with visions of monetary pursuit and material gain. Money is the ruling principle of *Treasure Island,* and the reader is hardly surprised to discover at the end of the book that the treasure is an epitome of all the world's currency: "English, French, Spanish, Portuguese, Georges, and Louises, doubloons and double guineas and moidores and sequins, the pictures of all the kings of Europe for the last hundred years, strange Oriental pieces stamped with what looked like wisps of string or bits of spider's web, round pieces and square pieces, and pieces bored through the middle, as if to wear them round your neck—nearly every variety of money in the world must, I think, have found a place in that collection . . ." (VI, 247).

Viewing *Treasure Island* as an economic myth serves to extend its psychological and social implications. By using the ingredients of conventional romance, it reconstructs with diagrammatic precision the ethical bones of Western society. Little distinction is drawn between the established possessors of respectable position and the cutthroat have-nots who lust for fame and power: both are motivated by the same underlying greed, a compulsive desire for material acquisition and self-aggrandizement. Moral lines are difficult to draw in such a world, and values are measured only by individual achievement. Its central figure is Silver who represents in his conduct the best possible method of survival. A utilitarian of the first order, he recognizes that he must survive by his wit and by his bluff. As Stevenson conceives him, he resembles Henley devoid of his finer qualities, a man dependent on "his strength, his courage, his quickness, and his magnificent geniality" ("My First Book: Treasure Island," VI, xxviii).

Always calculating, Long John Silver wins over even the cautious Livesey and the fearful Jim; ever mercurial, he sways between allegiance to Jim and an unsatiable desire for wealth. Silver's ambition goes beyond material gain, for he recognizes the power of money and hopes to invest it so that he may one day be a member of Parliament and ride through the streets in a coach. His whole being is directed toward the use of money to achieve reputation. A thorough pragmatist, he combats the difficulties of existence with whatever means at his disposal; a total individualist, he never forgets that his primary loyalty is to himself. Appropriately, he is the only one in the novel to emerge unscathed, to escape to a presumed life of comfort. While condemnation in the next world may well be his lot, his secular achievement is hardly impaired.

John Silver's complement is Jim Hawkins. Silver lives by his wits, but Jim moves in a world where luck is his protection; Silver is crafty, but Jim survives by accident and instinct. The best indication of their difference is in their individual reactions to the treasure hunt: Silver finds it a rousing adventure and a means to security; Jim sees the events as tragic and is condemned to such nightmares as he dreamt before. While Silver counts his gold, Jim reckons the lives lost upon the chase and forswears a like adventure. Just as Silver anticipates Stevenson's James Durie, Jim resembles his young David Balfour; both are the two faces of the Stevenson man. If Silver is the first of Stevenson's magnificent villains, Jim is the forerunner of his unheroic heroes. Unable to escape, he must make the best of his world, but only after realizing his inadequacies. At the end of his adventure, Jim is as much a prisoner as he was at Squire Trelawney's. Compelled to recount a story which he would rather forget, he serves as the voice of those who live his adventure with him and who, like him, are imprisoned in their memories.

The only true survivor of the treasure hunt is Silver, who leaves the known world and its aspirations for some supposed paradise with an old Negress and a pet parrot. In *Treasure Island,* such escape remains a remote possibility. The difficulty for romance occurs later when materialism shatters the purity of idealism and egoism brutalizes the charm of innocence. As an early romance, *Treasure Island* not only allows fantasy but spells out its ingredients with an artistry unparalleled in other works of its kind. Yet it neither sentimentalizes nor avoids the uglier aspects of the world it depicts. Like its author, it stands midway between a fanciful impulse toward romantic adventure and a necessary acknowledgement that the greatest adventure is the life we endure.

II The Black Arrow

Although not published in book form until 1888, *The Black Arrow* appeared in the pages of *Young Folks* in 1883 as a sequel to *Treasure Island*. Maintaining the pseudonym of Captain

George North, Stevenson responded to the editor's request for another boy's story with a tale of the War of the Roses which he always referred to as "tushery." [3] The readership of *Young Folks,* however, found it more to their liking than *Treasure Island;* and Stevenson acceded to popular taste by approving the book-length version. Yet *The Black Arrow* never again attained the popularity of its initial publication; most readers have either forgotten its existence or have read it with an eye toward its minor position among the novels.

The initial, favorable reception of the novel is nonetheless understandable for it is an exciting piece of historical re-creation whose eccentricities do not affect the quality of the adventure in quite the same way as they do in *Treasure Island.* Sharing with its predecessor certain characteristic Stevensonian variations from the norm, it touches lightly upon the ambiguities it introduces and concludes upon the happy ending it promises. At the same time, it lacks the depth of *Treasure Island;* and, instead of achieving a mythic timelessness, it is very much limited by its historical situation. Stevenson's use of history, in fact, explains many of the novel's limitations. Unlike the unspecified freedom of *Treasure Island* and the epic use of Scottish history in *Kidnapped* and *The Master of Ballantrae,* Stevenson is too much concerned in *The Black Arrow* with the routine details of the Medieval world and too closely influenced by his source, the Paston Letters. His characters are placed in a world in which they appear awkward because they are made to fit a historical context unsuited for them. The result is an intriguing play upon convention, an original view of the conflict between Lancaster and York whose action is forced, artificial in the way Stevenson dismissed it: the historical parody is obvious, and the moral complications are overly explicit.

The Black Arrow lacks the sweep of Stevenson's other historical adventures, although it offers a similar series of reversals. Things occur contrary to expectations, and people are tested continuously by their encumbering limitations. If historical particularity is its weakness, human sympathy is its strength. Richard Shelton, another of Stevenson's young idealists, finds himself unwillingly estranged from his former guardian, Sir Daniel Brackley, whom he now rightly suspects of his father's murder. Forced to flee Sir Daniel's authority, he aligns himself with the Yorkists whose politics he dislikes but whose protection he needs. Courageous in a clumsy sort of way, he finds partial favor with Richard Gloucester only to retreat behind his native unheroic values and retire to an Arcadian dwelling with his lady when he may be "apart from alarms in the green forest where their love began." The most surprising element in Richard's character is his inability to achieve his own purposes. From the beginning, he is dependent upon others: first upon Ellis Duckworth, the Robin-Hood figure whose avenging weapon gives the book its title, and then upon his love's lady-in-waiting (*mirabile dictu*) who helps him gain her hand. Although less dependent upon Fortune's whim than Jim Hawkins, Richard is just as strange a hero for a boy's adventure. It is one thing for Stevenson to raise the Hamlet question in a comic romance such as *Prince Otto*, to create an adult protagonist who has difficulty acting upon his intentions, but, in a historical adventure whose youthful audience thrives upon conclusive action, it is more than passing strange.

Such complications, however, rarely hinder the progress of the action. Richard's impulsive behavior is less damaging than it might have been; for, despite his ineptitude, matters right themselves, if not always with pleasing finality. The imbalance that remains, though interesting, seems too much a contrivance. The substitution of Yorkist authority for Lancastrian rule hardly promises a better world, nor does Ellis Duckworth's revenge upon Sir Daniel insure that the peasants will fare any better. Richard's inability to achieve Arblaster's forgiveness by saving his life forces home the bitter lesson that "a thing once done is not to be changed or remedied by any penitence." Rarely do such grim realities appear in a fiction dependent upon successful action. And yet, although the conventional morality of adventure fiction is challenged, it is not always possible to take the challenge seriously. Whereas in *Treasure Island* action and meaning were one, here they work against each other. The variations in *The Black Arrow* are striking, but too much so to be anything more than momentary.

III   Kidnapped

Romance takes still another turn in *Kidnapped*. While *Treasure Island* creates myth and *The Black Arrow* reproduces a Medieval pageant, *Kidnapped* resembles an epic set amid the turbulence

of Scottish history. As Stevenson's comic epic—its tragic equivalent is *The Master of Ballantrae*—it examines the troubled years
following the rebellion of 1845; but it draws back from its tragic
implications with the help of the romantic apparatus of boy's
adventure. While lacking the grimness of *The Master of Ballantrae, Kidnapped* is built upon a clash of loyalties no less significant for the history of its people. Its central issue is twofold:
David Balfour's struggle to claim his inheritance, and his Highland countrymen's struggle to preserve their land.

The time is six years after the ill-fated Jacobite rebellion, and
David Balfour, a young Lowlander of Highland stock, sets out
upon the death of his father to seek his uncle's ancestral home
and there gain his inheritance. His journey is short and unevent-
ful until he reaches his Uncle Ebenezer's decayed mansion which
turns out to be a cross between a Gothic parody and a Romantic
version of "Childe Roland" 's landscape, one complete with a
ruined tower. As expected, his uncle is the conventional, mean old
man of nursery tales who, instead of befriending David, attempts
to kill him. When this attempt proves unsuccessful, his uncle
has him kidnapped aboard the brig *Covenant* bound for the
Carolinas. On board, David encounters the renegade Highlander,
Alan Breck Stewart, and helps him prevail against the perfidious
ship's crew before the entire company is shipwrecked off the coast
of Mull.

The first part of David's adventures reads much like a typical
romance: still another quest by an orphan boy who must gain his
identity through personal achievement. Like Jim Hawkins and
Richard Shelton, David is alone in a world for which he is little
prepared; and he finds to his discomfort that its difficulties are
not easy to overcome. Saved from death upon his uncle's tower
by a fortunate heavenly illumination, he is tricked into boarding
the *Covenant* because of his boyish curiosity; capable of with-
standing armed men, he still displays the mawkish self-concern
of a Stevenson adolescent. These are, however, just incidentals,
the mechanisms by which events are set in motion.

Stevenson is concerned, however, with more than romantic
adventure; while utilizing its material, he develops a narrative
of epic proportions. David's mannerisms are not simply mani-
festations of his callowness but result from his Lowland education; his journey is not only into experience but into the interior

of the Highlands whose adherent he becomes; and his dependence is not upon a burly pirate nor a secretive champion but upon the flamboyant and vain Alan Breck, a figure out of history whose Highland ways and Highland loyalties he must accommodate to his own character. Finally, David's personal displacement is the event which transforms romantic adventure into national saga, for it signals the turn beyond David's own story to a depiction of his countrymen's enforced exile. As David's quest reverses itself so that he becomes the hunted, his adventure involves more than a simple search for identity.

Stevenson hints at things to come even before David enters the Highlands, most notably by naming the ship upon which he is taken captive the *Covenant,* and by manning it with a captain who is far from the expected one-dimensional villain. The name *Covenant* suggests not only the central document of Scottish history for which so much blood was shed and by which Scotland achieved a short-lived independence but also the very foundation of the ethical context from which David emerges. Unlike the *Hispaniola,* whose name retains all the romance of Spanish frigates and pirate gold, the *Covenant* is a mixture of glory and sadness—a reminder of past achievements amid a realization of present dishonor. Captain Hoseason, its chief officer, is likewise of mixed qualities. Directly responsible for cashiering David, he nonetheless behaves so well toward his captive that even the priggish David admits the Captain "was two men, and left the better one behind as soon as he set foot aboard the vessel." (In *Catriona,* the reader learns that Hoseason is thought to be the most loyal skipper in the trade.) Never remiss in paying his respects to his mother whenever he sails past her home, and ever constant in his religious devotions as befits the church-goer he is, Hoseason adds a touch of moral ambiguity to the first part of David's adventures which contrasts with the histrionics of Uncle Ebenezer.

Not until after the shipwreck, however, do events turn away from romance and toward Scottish history. Even the appearance of Alan Breck Stewart aboard the *Covenant* barely prepares the reader for the subsequent action. Before the chase in the Highlands, Alan Breck is confined to his romantic trappings; only when he and David flee the pursuing English army does he become the father that David lost and the brother he never had.

The central section of the narrative is a brilliant example of how romantic adventure can be joined with historical detail to create a national epic. The major event of this part of *Kidnapped* is the Appin murder. After the wreck, David makes his way first to the islet of Earraid (where he has the embarrassing experience of mistaking high tide for a perpetual barrier to the mainland) and then into the interior of the Highlands to meet once more with Alan Breck. Shortly before the two find each other, David is witness to the murder of Colin Campbell, known as the "Red Fox" because of his oppressive policy toward his countrymen in the name of his English masters. Thought to be involved in the murder,[4] David and Alan Breck are forced to flee farther into the mountains until their journey becomes a virtual circuit of the Highland country. As both endure physical hardship and personal antagonism, they grow in mutual understanding and dependence.

The events of this central portion have led at least one critic to compare *Kidnapped* with Mark Twain's *Huckleberry Finn*. Both are tales of pursuit in which a young boy, much against his social conscience, befriends an outlawed member of society and joins him in flight. Whether or not Stevenson actually used Twain's book as his model, he clearly wished to depict a similar developmental pattern.[5] David is loyal to king and country. The son of a schoolmaster and the protegé of a strict constructionist, he emerges from his upbringing a conventional Lowlander. His journey to his uncle's estate is a natural assertion of legal and moral decorum. Thus, when he encounters the proscribed Alan Breck, representing all that is inimical to his given values, he barely knows how to proceed. Relying upon his instinctive goodness, David befriends Alan Breck and becomes his confidant and eventual benefactor.

As they travel the wilds of the Highland country, David learns about his ancestral heritage, not as measured by the money his uncle would cheat him of, but by the blood he shares with those of his countrymen who now must mask their lives under compliance to a rule which hardly enables them to be men. His meeting with such persons as Cluny, the robber chieftain, whose sense of honor is all that remains to him; Robin Oig, who valiantly accompanied his father Rob Roy on many an exploit, and whose prowess is now reduced to dueling upon the pipes; and James Stewart, who as present leader of his clan can hardly feed his family (and whose fate it is to be convicted and hanged for the Appin murder), convinces David that his provincial education has indeed been partial.

Yet the purpose of *Kidnapped* is to provide more than a lesson in maturation. Rather than establish a division between the moral value of geographical areas as does *Huck Finn*, the novel attempts to reconcile differences by establishing the common humanity of a ravaged people. There are few more poignant cries than those David hears coming from an emigrant ship as he first makes his way to meet Alan, a ship that represents a reality which makes his uncle's attempt at kidnapping simply a child's nightmare. The enforced separation of families that was a daily occurrence to the Highlanders, the emasculation of former warriors, the uprooting of native peoples, the loss of all that is meant by homeland are lessons David must acquire and keep with him when called upon to aid his countrymen. Unlike Huck, David never considers "lighting out for the territory," for he realizes that his fate is allied with his native history.

David is not the sole beneficiary of his journey. Alan Breck receives not only a lesson in moral tolerance and physical endurance but also the means by which he may escape to freedom. More flamboyant than effectual, his vanity is as limiting as David's self-centeredness. His marked displays of affectation (a reduction of heroic grandeur) is a sad comment on the necessary posturing of the Highlander. Beneath his bluster, however, he is a brave soldier and a true loyalist whose reward is to be banished from his native land. His journey is one into exile in which all he can do is leave behind some part of his legacy to David—an inheritance far more meaningful than the estate David eventually attains.

By the time David and Alan find their way back to Edinburgh, the business of David's monetary inheritance has been largely forgotten. Indeed, as Mr. Rankeillor makes clear after listening to David's story, the significant part of the narrative has already passed: "Well, well . . . this is a great epic, a great Odyssey of yours." Yet, unlike Ithaca, Scotland cannot be put together upon the return of its wanderers. The conclusion, therefore, turns from history back to romance. After the monumental journey through Scottish history and landscape, the final action in which Ebenezer is made to admit his complicity in David's kidnapping

cannot but appear anticlimactic. Unable to reverse history, Stevenson must call upon his narrative powers to offer pleasant
fiction in place of unpleasant actuality. David becomes the lord
of Shaw's, but his title is far less valuable than the struggle to
achieve it.

IV David Balfour

Catriona (American name: *David Balfour*) is a logical sequel
to *Kidnapped,* a mundane equivalent of its epical grandeur.
Never so popular as its predecessor, it turns the sweep of Scottish
history into a catalogue of petty intrigue and personal jealousy.
The other side of romance, it solidifies present realities by reducing human action to a series of groping gestures lessening much
of the humor in the human comedy. In *Catriona,* hesitation becomes equivocation, and self-centeredness is a resignation of
responsibility. Just as Stevenson refrained from pursuing the
tragic implications of *Kidnapped,* he here is perhaps too intent
on revealing the pitiful banality of the commonplace.

Again, Stevenson's use of history limits his choice. Wishing to
continue the issues raised in *Kidnapped,* he chooses as his central
incident the trial of James of the Glen; and by so doing he establishes an immediate barrier to his narrative success. The details
of that trial were too well known for him to disguise them in
fictional contrivance. Since Stevenson could not avoid the actuality of James's death, it occurs shortly after the middle of the
narrative; and, from that point, the action leads downward toward the matter-of-fact conclusion in which, with dreary ex-
pectancy, the Lowland David and the Highland Catriona are
married. Having plunged immediately into the commonplace of
history, Stevenson cannot romanticize its dreary inevitability.

Taken together, therefore, *Kidnapped* and *Catriona* illustrate
fiction's complex role toward history: as romance which pushes
the actual toward myth and epic; as realism which reduces the
heroic to concrete depiction of man's insignificance. David Balfour changes little throughout the novels because he is a figure
of both worlds. His maturity occurs only after he reflects upon
his past, and it manifests itself only as he narrates his experience
to his children. As he relives his adventures, he recognizes that
fiction is necessary to a history which remembers failure more

than achievement: truly a sight to make angels laugh and men weep.

V *Comic Romances*

The Wrong Box (1889) and *Prince Otto* (1885) share the distinction of being possibly the least read of Stevenson's novels— even the critics have chosen to neglect them. As examples of comic romance, they are neither so inventive nor so successful as the *New Arabian Nights*, for they lack its whimsical antics and charming artifice. The subject matter in both novels is banal, the actors too much like real people, and the humor too much a part of the world it attempts to parody. In short, both novels are not sufficiently fantastic to serve as romance nor sufficiently caustic to serve as social comedy. They waver halfway between the two, serving as examples of how even the complete may remain unfinished. Occasionally funny, *The Wrong Box* is a mild gibe at commercial speculation, while *Prince Otto* offers a rustic harlequinade of Shakespearian material.

Stevenson's failures, however, often provide interesting commentary upon his more successful fiction. As a gloss upon romance and comedy, *The Wrong Box* and *Prince Otto* reveal the delicate hand necessary to achieve either; they also reveal the seeming incompatibility between the two. With other forms of fantasy, romance shares an indisposition toward laughter, a knowledge that a shattering reality lies in comedy. Stevenson's skepticism, however, forced him toward exactly the ambivalence which such a combination necessitates: incapable of believing (despite himself) in the possibility of romance and unwilling to adopt the pessimism of comedy, he attempted to write fiction which would maintain an imperative optimism while it laughed at the posture. *Prince Otto*, even more than *The Wrong Box*, is the result of this attempt—an impulse toward laughter whose roots are within an anguished sense of self-limitation.

While the ingenious misadventures of the Finsburys as they bumble their way through the complications of *The Wrong Box* are often delightful, *Prince Otto* is clearly a more substantial novel. *The Wrong Box* resembles a Mack Sennett farce; *Prince Otto* reads like a Marx Brothers scenario, something out of *Duck Soup* without its anarchistic mayhem. The setting conjures up a make-believe kingdom, Grunewald (straight out of *As You Like*

It)—"Under the greenwood tree/ Who loves to lie with me?"—
whose ruler is a cross between the banished Duke of that play
and Prince Florizel of *The Winter's Tale*. Otto is from the outset
a prince-errant, a vagrant from the responsibilities of office. Having all but abdicated his throne, he wanders in disguise among
his people, basking in their affection but shamed by his reputation as a cuckold. Finally called to defend his honor, he makes
ineffectual gestures while realizing that his passivity has already
gone too far to be redeemed. At the end, he regains his wife but
loses his throne, and he retires to his wished-for forest retreat to
compose poetry like his historical counterpart, Charles of Orleans.

Heir to the Bohemian artifice of *The Winter's Tale* and the
pastoral idealism of *As You Like It*, Otto is also a ruler with an
unenviable resemblance to Hamlet. With little intent to disguise
either his Shakespearian relationships or his symbolic role, Stevenson places him in Mittwalden (a middle world between this
one and the next), a forest of Arden removed from life's turbulence and seemingly isolated from the intrusions of a rude society.
Otto is Stevensonian man elevated to the throne, a Will O' the
Mill given regal authority and allowed to display his gnawing
ineffectuality. In fact, it is not surprising that *Prince Otto* was
Stevenson's "last effort of his earliest manner" (Preface, VII, xv),
for it resembles a fictionalized essay in which characters do not
interact with each other so much as illustrate particular attitudes
toward action: Otto retreats from action, Gondremark attempts
to manipulate it to his satisfaction, Seraphina is duped by her
inability to evaluate it correctly, and Countess Von Rosen meets
it head on and accepts its necessity. The Countess' role is especially significant since she is the true activist individual who,
despite questionable means, achieves her goals by a willful compulsion to persevere. Von Rosen is not so much a woman—Stevenson always had difficulty creating believable women—as a force
powering her way through the novel. She is the adversary to all
of Otto's pretensions, and she forces him to become a man even if
his being so means the loss of his kingdom.

As Shakespearian offspring, with Meredithian blessing, *Prince
Otto* fixes with unerring precision Stevenson's difficulty as a
writer of fiction—a difficulty muted by his greater success in his
other novels. Caught between romance and realism, he attempts
to satisfy both—and glaringly illustrates his dilemma. Otto's pre-

dicament as artist-king is essentially Stevenson's. No wonder that, according to Lloyd, "some of the chapters he re-wrote as many as seven times; [and] of all his books, save *The Master of Ballantrae* —and, later, *Weir,* it was the closest to his heart" (Introduction, VII, xi). Though Otto was originally modeled after his cousin, Robert Mowbray Stevenson, Robert Louis evidently incorporated into his character much of himself. An example of that sedulous imitation which Stevenson describes as his literary practice, Otto emerges as a Stevenson man, a suitable relation to all his infirm heroes who attempt to retreat into an Edenic forest and who succeed at best only as they relive their experience in artistic creation.

VI   The Master of Ballantrae, Weir of Hermiston, St. Ives

Stevenson's three Scottish novels—*The Master of Ballantrae* (1889), *Weir of Hermiston* (1894), and *St. Ives* (1897)—were all written during successive stages of his growing realization that he would remain forever in exile. Accordingly, each represents, at least partially, a sentimental look backward. In addition, two of the three—*The Master of Ballantrae* and *Weir of Hermiston*—indicate increased artistic maturity, an ability to handle narrative material with a sophistication not always evident previously. Yet, as is often the case with Stevenson, limitations remain. He completed only one of the novels, *The Master of Ballantrae,* and that at much cost. Therefore, despite Quiller-Couch's addition to *St. Ives* and Colvin's "editorial note" about the supposed conclusion of *Weir,* only *The Master* can be discussed with any certainty.[6] If *Weir of Hermiston* promised to be his masterpiece, the promise remains unfulfilled; and *The Master of Ballantrae* must stand as the fullest achievement of Stevenson's narrative art. Often described as a fragmented novel whose complexity eludes Stevenson, it is on the contrary an intricately developed narrative whose chilling tone and distant adventures are prepared for from the beginning.[7]

The difficulty in *The Master* is not its narrative structure but its multiple ambivalences, for no other of Stevenson's works is so charged with the burden of his paradoxical attitudes and no other of his novels certainly is so dramatically inconclusive. David Daiches' belief, as expressed in *Stevenson and the Art of Fiction* (11), that in *Prince Otto* Stevenson attempted to include more than the form could hold, is applicable as well to *The Master* —but with a difference. In *Prince Otto,* Stevenson confronted a problem in which the fragile structure of comic romance could not sustain the weight of the philosophical ideas he wished to convey. In *The Master,* on the other hand, the fictional medium and its thematic values are far better integrated; but skepticism is so inescapably present throughout the novel that no fictional structure could be true to Stevenson's unbelief and still satisfy the reader. Of all his works, it is the only one he repeatedly referred to as a tragedy; and it shares with *The Ebb-Tide* as grim a view of life as he allowed himself to present.

Stevenson's use of history, along with his narrative sophistication, marks the advance *The Master* represents. While *The Ebb-Tide* shares its pessimism, *Kidnapped* is its more appropriate analogue, for both their historical setting and their epic magnitude identify them as related studies in Scottish history. Though similar in kind, however, they differ in degree. As M. R. Ridley points out in his introduction to the Everyman edition of *The Master of Ballantrae* and *Weir of Hermiston* (1956): "*Kidnapped* is a romance, a story of events, and well though many of the characters are drawn, it is not what they are, but what happens to them, that holds the interest. But *The Master* is first and foremost a study of characters, and the events, exciting as they are, are almost incidental, important only for the light they throw on new aspects of the characters" (x).

Scottish history is not a background against which characters perform their tasks, but a vital process which informs the very blood of those who are its captives. In *The Master,* history and fiction correspond; character and event are joined so that event becomes the direct motivation for action. Stylistically, *The Master* is not only *Kidnapped*'s analogue but its antithesis: the latter uses epic allusion to develop the possibility of heroic adventure, but the former parodies heroic action with a series of incidents uncompromising in their denial of achievement: either present success or future redemption.

In none of Stevenson's other novels—with the possible exception of *Weir*—are narrative action and narrative structure as complementary. Domestic strife is made to mirror national strife, and brother is set against brother in much the same way as Jacobite opposes Whig. The entire movement of *The Master* is built upon

a correspondence between the larger world at war with itself
and its effect upon the dissolution of an ancient family. The
Duries of Durisdeer have descended from their storied position
in Scottish legend to compromise and temporizing. Once a fabled
part of their country's folklore, they are now reduced to maintaining a semblance of their former glory by shameful appease-
ment and contrived alliance. The first in the line of descent is the
present Lord Durisdeer who has neglected his paternal duties
by favoring one of his sons to the virtual exclusion of the other
and who has withdrawn from his responsibilities by allowing his
favored son to take command both of his affection and his duties.
He presides over a household which, like the Finsburys' in *The
Wrong Box*, contains "a family in appearance, in reality a financial association." As the "banker" of the association, Lord Durisdeer's security depends upon the good currency of Alison Graeme,
his orphaned ward, who brings with her the financial means by
which he may insure his stability.

The victims of Lord Durisdeer's mismanagement are his sons,
James and Henry. James is the favored older son and, as such,
possesses the title of "Master" until his presumed death. As Stevenson depicts him, he is, to use his creator's own words, "all I
know of the devil" (Letters, III, 36). A combination of Byronic
gesture and Satanic malevolence, he is the most dashing of Stevenson's activist scoundrels, a stunning example of the moral
dilemma that his presence forces upon the novel. Outwardly attractive, his egotism feeds upon the cunning which he employs
to satisfy its appetite. A near relation of Milton's Satan, to whom
he is compared, he shares all the ambivalences which the post-
Blakeian romantics imposed upon the traditional figure of evil.
Truly a "master" at deceit, he lives upon his ability to command
all as his retainers, achieving a loyalty unquestioning in its ac-
quiescence. When the Stuart rebellion forces him to declare his
allegiance, he defies reasonable action and family responsibility
by turning moral choice into a game of chance, and upon the
toss of a coin rides out to fight upon the losing side. Ever crafty,
he insures his own safety by turning spy, while continuing to
thrive as a parasite upon his family's finances and his friends'
affection. Temporarily sustained by his deceptions, he finally
cannot save himself from his brother's unremitting hatred. At the
end of the novel, he becomes Henry's prey in a fearful chase

which begins among the vestigial remains of a ruined Scotland and concludes in the primeval wilderness of a barren America.

As befits his Satanic role, James is an incubus. Driven by an insatiable desire to revenge himself upon his brother, he "takes possession" of Henry, turning him into a creature much like himself, but devoid of surface charm. As James grows more dominant, Henry becomes a sinister figure of destructive malice, the embodiment of raw hatred stripped of its protective tissue. An average man ("neither very bad nor yet very able, but an honest, solid sort of lad like his neighbors"), Henry is forced into an all-consuming hatred by his inability to withstand the pressures of personal responsibility and familial obligation. Initially a sympathetic sufferer of parental neglect, he becomes a pitiful embodiment of Blake's Poison Tree as he nurtures his resentment so that its "fruits" produce nothing but death for him and his brother. Whatever he does, Henry is unable to escape the constant menacing presence of The Master; even supposed death cannot reduce James's influence. Henry gains his brother's title, but he never attains the love of his father, his wife (James's former fiancée), or any who remain loyal to his brother's memory. Plagued by his inability to become The Master in anything but name, he succumbs to James's fatal attraction by becoming a more ardent disciple of evil than James himself. Limited by his galling mediocrity, Henry dedicates himself finally to a maddened attempt to exorcise his brother's powers only to recognize that the incubus has already taken full possession of his being.

The measure of Henry's decline is nowhere better gauged than in the changing attitudes of the novel's major narrator, the faithful steward Mackellar. Stevenson's use of Mackellar as both narrative voice and moral norm indicates his increased powers, for Mackellar allows him a perspective through the eyes of a speaker who is not a direct participant in the action. Beginning as a faithful partisan of Henry's, Mackellar, for all his loyalty, cannot disguise his growing attraction to James; and his increasing suspicion that his Master is no longer the man he once was emphasizes the progress of Henry's decline. Stevenson carefully sketches him as a comic variant of both brothers: on the one hand, a coward with an abundance of Henry's defeatism, he is also, on the other hand, much like James in his determination. Central to the novel's success, he provides a necessary comment on its action, both as dominant voice and as the spokesman for its unresolved moral ambiguity. Caught between James's magnetism and Henry's pitiful isolation, he finds himself an unwilling loyalist of both; and his final act is to unite the brothers under a single monument signifying their inescapable identity.

Mackellar's moral uncertainties are Stevenson's as well. Just as *The Master* represents his advance as a novelist, it also represents his advance as a moralist. Ambiguity does not always signal positive action, but for Stevenson it here signifies an honesty which in the past he often attempted to mute behind stylistic pyrotechnics. Instead, he forces into the present narrative an array of past motifs and past characters in order to construct a compendium of his former devices; and the foremost of these is the treasure hunt. Like similar pursuits in his past fiction, the lure of gold helps to keep the narrative together—James buries his treasure on his first visit to upstate New York so that he may return some day and reclaim it—while it provides an ironic reversal upon any expected successful result.

Yet here, more than before, its inclusion is gratuitous; for Stevenson hardly needed it as a unifying force; fraternal hatred is a sufficient lure to bring both brothers into the American wilderness. It is here simply because it is superfluous, a fictional anachronism in a novel no longer directed to the creation of myth or to the re-creation of historical event. *Treasure Island* and *Kidnapped* are examples of how boy's adventure can transcend its apparent limitations but neither is sufficient for what Stevenson attempts to do in *The Master*. As Stevenson passes beyond the pictorial into a dramatic study of character, he discards simple adventure for a more profound use of romance. The quest in *The Master* is no longer for mere treasure but for the material of life itself.

Similarly Teach, the bombastic sham pirate, and Alan Breck, the foppish rebel, must confront James and be defeated in their attempts to best him. Alan Breck, who first encounters James at the beginning of his wanderings, challenges him to a horse race in much the same manner that he challenged Robin Oig to a duel upon the pipes. But, though the stakes are as trivial, James obeys none of the gentlemanly code necessary to maintain honor. After an inimical exchange of words, he bolts forward upon his horse without giving Alan a chance to mount; indeed, he even forces

Alan to become his own horse as he chases after him on foot. In leaving him behind, James asserts a new code whose "rules" are based solely upon self-loyalty and whose "honor" is measured by whatever means are necessary to achieve personal satisfaction. What Alan stands for is reduced to a series of empty gestures which have little value in the modern world. Beneath Alan's affectations there remains a loyalty which never wavers in its allegiance to clan and to country; beneath James's attractiveness there seethes a passion so headstrong that it knows only its own vindictiveness.

Teach is a like victim of The Master's treachery. Initially James's captor, he soon becomes his captive as James reveals Teach's histrionics to be nothing more than air, a measure of his ability to grimace fearfully. The evil Teach represents is nothing more than play, which is innocent in comparison with the calculated egotism which The Master displays. Teach is a figure out of boy's adventure, an undeveloped Silver who has neither his respectable demeanor nor his crafty abilities. Silver indeed begins the tradition which culminates in The Master; for, magnetic in their ability to charm others, they have little care for any but themselves. Yet James is considerably more dangerous: Silver is a commonplace villain with conventional ambitions; James's evil is elemental rather than commonplace, and his ambition, were it to become conventional, would signal the advent of a Hobbesian world.

As Stevenson paced the verandah of his cabin at Saranac, looking out at the landscape whose winter chill dominates the novel, he could not help but be alternately grieved and gratified by the direction of his fiction. While he was better able to handle the intricacies of narrative form, he was less able to allow his virtuosity to mask an essential pessimism. The extended movement of the action from the Old World to the New, from Scotland to India to America, reinforces a continuity of human depravity, an unchanging cycle of selfish motive and savage behavior which Stevenson could not disguise. Subtitled *A Winter's Tale*, *The Master of Ballantrae* is an epic without heroic action. It concludes amid the deathlike snow of an American wilderness, which appropriately signifies the emptiness of final possibility. After the New World has proved a wasteland much like the old, after men behave there with the brutality of their old-world counterparts, the hopefulness of life reaches its final bounds. Stevenson sets that limit with his grimmest reminder of mortality. Threatened with murder for his treasure, James attempts to play with death by using an old Indian trick taught him by his servant, Secundra Dass, but it proves too feeble. Even as Henry sees his brother dead, he succumbs to the emptiness of an achieved passion. Upon the flickering of James's eyelids which he believes suggestive of his brother's indestructibility, Henry falls dead upon the ground, a partner in death of the brother he wished to deny in life.

Throughout the writing of *The Master*, Stevenson worried about the conclusion. He feared it was out of keeping with the tone and the substance of the previous action, and he often referred to it as melodramatic. Although undeniably melodramatic, it is appropriately so. The ending of *The Master* turns melodrama on its head by using its devices to create unexpected results. Melodrama thrives on its ability to turn suggestion into action, to offer the possibilities of make-believe for the limitations of reality. The conclusion of *The Master* reverses this direction. It offers reality where one expects possibility, and it insures limitation by relating the death of its protagonists not only to the downfall of a noble family but to the demise of a once-great nation. In order to do so, Stevenson works with the very material whose assumptions he transcends. His success in *Treasure Island* and *Kidnapped* is a prelude to his ability in *The Master* to take romance beyond the confines of daydream.

As early as 1878, in his series of essays entitled *Edinburgh: Picturesque Notes*, Stevenson foreshadowed the mood of his final novels: "There is no Edinburgh emigrant, far or near . . . but he or she carries some lively pictures of the mind . . . indelible in the memory and delightful to study in the intervals of toil" (II, 330). In later years, with few intervals from toil, he found himself a model of that emigrant banished by ill health and forbidden to return to the land whose memory he cherished. While Scotland as place and as national monument plays a major role in his other two Scottish novels, it does so in varying degree.

St. Ives is little more than a well-made novel set in and around Edinburgh so that Stevenson could vicariously revisit those familiar places of his childhood. Even without Quiller-Couch's inferior conclusion, it holds little promise to be the kind of novel *Weir* remains. Of all his Scottish stories, it is most tangentially related to its surroundings. *Weir*, on the contrary, is born from the native ballad, rooted in the Scottish countryside, and recalls the primitive passions and the tragic fate of its national origins. Like the Weaver's Stone whose legend broods over the novel as an unavoidable reminder of national and personal tragedy, the lives of all its characters are intermingled not only with each other but with a doom which has descended upon an entire people.

"The voice of generations dead" echoes through the pages of *Weir*. Each of the novel's characters—Adam Weir, his wife Jean, his son Archie, his housekeeper Kirstie, her nephews "the four black brothers of Cauldstaneslap," and their sister Christina—are entangled in their present history and their past heritage that is no less complex, no less influential. Throughout the novel there is an inescapable feeling that all has happened before, that its participants are acting out a repetition of what legend has determined as inevitable action. Archie Weir's first rendezvous with Christina Elliot at the Praying Weaver's Stone is not only a troth of their love but a mutual pledge to accept their disparate ancestry. Through them runs the villainous blood of the Rutherfords, the savage compulsion of Adam Weir, and the primitive heroism of the Clan Ellwald. Familial and national destiny rules the novel like a pagan fate: "uncontrolled by any Christian deity, obscure, lawless and august—moving indissolubly in the affairs of Christian men." No longer are Stevenson's characters limited by their fancy, or by a narrow society which forbids personal freedom: the people of *Weir* are captives of their destiny, a power which insures failure in the very act of being human. This sense of inescapable history Stevenson has in mind when he writes in the middle of Kirstie's description: "For that is the mark of the Scot of all classes: that he stands in an attitude towards the past unthinkable to Englishmen, and remembers and cherishes the memory of his forbears, good or bad; and there burns alive in him a sense of identity with the dead even to the twentieth generation" (XXVIII, 63).

At the time of his death, Stevenson had completed *Weir* sufficiently to indicate that Archie and Christina were to become the victims of their tragic destiny. No matter what action he might have chosen for the novel's conclusion, he had already directed his narrative toward tragedy. Archie and Christina meet in the rustic isolation of a fabled countryside, but their meeting is first prepared for among the decaying elegance of Edinburgh's George Square. Archie comes to Hermiston, his family's country estate, after a falling-out with his father that is so serious that the Justice-Clerk banishes his son from his presence until he learns to be a man and not an "eediot." Reared by his pious and timid mother, Archie inherits not only her naiveté but her fear and incomprehension of her husband. He grows up with a hatred tempered by a smug self-righteousness which holds out forgiveness as a privilege. What he must learn is that he is more his father's son than he would admit—that he is indeed a child of the Adam Weir who carries in him a piece of the "adamantine Adam" which the Justice-Clerk displays with such vehemence.

Yet, like most of Stevenson's novels, *Weir of Hermiston* is a *bildungsroman* with a difference; for Archie Weir's introduction to life is more substantial than a mere lesson in experience. More than any of his other novels, in fact, *Weir* captures the essential frustrations of maturity, for it indicates that "education" is primarily a process where one is taught to suppress basic instincts. As Archie comes to recognize his kinship with his father, he realizes the "aboriginal savageness" which his father has bequeathed him and learns that civilization is but a modern re-enactment of an ancient script.

Weir of Hermiston is a study of frustration. One may call the force that frustrates pagan fate or Christian curse, but man is prevented from achieving his desires by a force so much a part of his being that he can no more escape it than he can his own identity. This message is what Stevenson has been working toward in his previous writings, the focal point of his didactic essays and his allegorical fiction. In *Weir*, he takes it off the scaffold and into the structure. The Lord Justice-Clerk, modeled after the actual Lord Braxfield, is an elemental force who approaches his legal role with a savagery which barely disguises the organized butchery of his legality. Forced to repress his essential being, he manipulates man's law in order to satisfy nature's drives. The elder Kirstie is much like her employer: a "moorland Helen" who retains her voluptuousness even into middle age, she is an earth-mother whose potential fecundity remains unrealized. "Destined to be the bride of heroes and the mother of their children," she becomes instead the caretaker of a romantic heritage and the keeper of an eternal desire.

The hallmark of Stevenson's maturity is exactly that moral candor which is essential to *Weir*. As a novelist, his narrative apparatus is romance; but his philosophical conclusions often mirror those of the realists whose crude effects he disparaged. Working from assumptions clearly distinct from theirs, and developing narratives directed away from their rigidity, he arrives at a view of life no more hopeful than that which he finds in them. The difference, however, for him is that, if the achievement is not to be, the pursuit may at least prove rewarding. His novels, therefore, often suggest the playfulness of game and the wistfulness of artifice; but, like the underlying barbarism of civilization, beneath the surface of his romance lies the grim specter of inevitable failure.

Weir of Hermiston would undoubtedly have been the epitome of this paradox. Perhaps this recognition has caused critics to consider this novel his highest achievement. The pageantry of heroic adventure, the epic grandeur of national struggle, the savage repression of a semicivilized people, the thwarted love and unrealized ambition that Stevenson built into parts of his previous fiction are incorporated into every part of *Weir of Hermiston*. It was to be the culmination of all the fictional machinery and moral problems with which he wrestled in his other novels, but it remains a record of a struggle unresolved. Like the "willful convulsion of brute nature" upon which it elliptically concludes, *Weir of Hermiston* bursts upon the world full blown but dies a premature death. Revealing unquestionable promise, it remains a testament to Stevenson's ability to mature not only as a moralist but as a serious writer of romance. Yet the novel also serves as a graphic reminder that successful achievement may indeed be an impossibility both in and out of fiction.

VII *The New World*

While both *The Wrecker* (1892) and *The Ebb-Tide* (1894) were written in collaboration with Lloyd Osbourne, they are strikingly representative of Stevenson's emotions during his final years.[8] To anyone who has followed the progress of his fiction, these works represent the logical conclusion to the romance he tried to write, for they end in nothingness: in a structural void which begins and ends nowhere, and upon an uncharted island whose savior is a Jonathan Edwards come to life again in the Pacific.

The Wrecker is *Treasure Island* grown up; and, like an adult version of a childish vision, it turns gay insouciance into vapid banality. As Stevenson admits in the novel's dedicatory epilogue, it is "full of the need and the lust of money, so that there is scarce a page in which the dollars do not jingle . . ." (XXI, 421). Yet rarely has lust for anything appeared so trivial. Before the novel concludes, the reader learns that the supposedly valuable wreck is really a worthless hulk whose "value" is a matter of personal honor, a quality strangely out of place in the world of this novel. The commercial spirit, though still impulsive, is no longer capable of an adventure like *Treasure Island*. Stevenson's attempt to bring romance into the modern world results in failure.

In the Epilogue, Stevenson explains the method by which he and Lloyd attempted to structure the novel. Their primary attraction was to the open-endedness of the modern mystery which "consists in beginning your yarn anywhere but at the beginning, and finishing it anywhere but at the end." Whether they succeeded or not, the attempt alone offers a glimpse of a Stevenson less sure of the necessity to follow a narrative line from the beginning (see letter to Barrie, IV, 126). *The Wrecker* represents his refusal to work with a fixed structure in a world in which it is no longer so relevant.

Certainly the teleology which he imposes upon his other narratives, and which he often had difficulty realizing, is here no longer a moral issue. The structure of *Treasure Island* resembles the map which was its inspiration, a clearly plotted line in a direction which ends in the expected location, if not with the promised result. The treasure map becomes a key metaphor for the novel, for it combines the romance of money with the details of its acquisition. The world it reflects, though hanging upon frivolous values, is still capable of producing adventure, of sending men off on a hunt whose attraction is infectious and enduring. In *The Wrecker,* by extending the gesture of adventure into the commonplace world of everyday trivia, Stevenson reduces the treasure hunt to a business enterprise and the treasure to a product of commercial investment. As the map becomes a contract, deliberate details become diffused within a narrative whose structure reflects its inconclusive action. In *Treasure Island,* Stevenson succeeds in lifting the commercial spirit into a myth of Western aspiration; here he succeeds equally well in destroying that myth. "The Wrecker" might very well be an epithet for its creator as well as a metaphor for the dismal emptiness upon which the narrative of *The Flying Scud* comes to rest.

Stevenson so structures the novel that it consistently works against itself. Filled with a sweeping change of locale—included are memories of Paris, Barbizon, California, and the Tropics—it builds up a brilliant panorama of expectation only to conclude upon the ethereality of a burst bubble. Promising enormous riches, it laughs at its own pretensions by exposing its artificial suspense. Structured upon epic proportions, it depends for its strength upon the precision of vignette and the accuracy of reminiscence. Though Stevenson's longest novel, it is memorable primarily for its brief effects: a picture of early San Francisco or of Loudon Dodd as he surveys the luminous horizon and muses upon his link with ancient man.

Loudon Dodd is the major character in a book where characterization is purposely hurried, a sharp stroke rather than a detailed portrait. His primary function is to embody the conflicting values which oscillate throughout the novel. As a would-be artist, he attempts to defy his materialist ethos by breaking away from its environs and assuming a new life in France. The more he attempts to create, however, the more unsuccessful he becomes, and the more dependent he grows on his millionaire father. The beginning of his commercial surrender occurs when he accepts his father's commission for a statue to grace the capitol of his native country. From that point on he abandons his artistic pursuits for a life of commercial speculation and becomes allied first with Jim Pinkerton, with whom he engages to salvage the supposedly valuable wreck, and then with Carthew, the indolent nobleman who protects his reputation by making Loudon his financial agent. At the end of his adventures, Loudon is comfortable for life with someone else's money; and he has become little more than a parasite. His role is to represent his patron, and his identity is lost in that role: "He runs me now. It's all his money."

As the protagonist in an adult *Treasure Island,* Loudon is appropriately a Jim Hawkins grown up. Dependent on circumstance to set him right, and never capable of achieving his desired goal, he is a pawn in a game far more serious and damaging than Jim's adventures. Jim cavorts among creatures of fantasy; Loudon plays the "money game." Successful neither as artist nor as entrepreneur, Loudon remains a second-rate sycophant who is secure so long as he never chases after treasure again. His story is perhaps as pitiable a record of failure as Stevenson presented in any novel, for his life is one of complete submission. It is indeed the pathetic equivalent of the tragedy which immediately preceded it in *Scribner's Magazine;* for, despite its gloom, *The Master of Ballantrae* concludes upon a promise of reconciliation, even if in death. No such promise exists in *The Wrecker,* no sense of tragic irony. Positing a world in which objects are thought to have value, Stevenson mocks man's assumptions by reducing its promise to a worthless hulk foundering in an unfathomable sea.

Foundering is the characteristic action of *The Ebb-Tide* as well, but men not ships threaten to sink to the bottom. As the last work to be published before Stevenson's death, it might well be considered as a fitting epitaph to his literature and to his philosophy. A striking parallel to the stridently heroic words which decorate his tomb, it is nothing less than the death cry of romance, an apocalyptic vision where daydream is turned to nightmare and El Dorado becomes the pestilential domain of a maniacal dictator. More than his other novels, *The Ebb-Tide* is mired in a cesspool of civilized values. Its characters are literally and figuratively "on the beach," and the apathetic degeneracy which they display is considerably more frightening than the crudest manifestation of legendary evil.

The three beachcombers who constitute the trio of the first part of the book and Attwater, who adds an all-too-harmonious note to the final quartet, represent the depths to which the human species is capable of sinking. Stevenson repeatedly described the novel as "a black, ugly, trampling, violent story" (Letters, III, 181); "a dreadful, grimy business in the third person" (Letters, IV, 189); "a most grim and gloomy tale" (Letters, IV, 160). Upon its completion, he confessed to Colvin the physical and mental strain which its composition had demanded: "Well, it's done. Those tragic 16 pp. are at last finished, and I have put away thirty-two pages of chips, and have spent thirteen days about as nearly in Hell as a man could expect to live through. It's done, and of course it ain't worth while, and who cares? There it is, and about as grim a tale as was ever written, and as grimy, and as hateful" (Letters, IV, 184).

Stevenson sets the mood with a series of visual symbols graphic in their depiction of human depravity: physical illness mirrors spiritual disease; men are reduced to beastly scavengers who devour their food like hounds; and temporary refuge to nurse their ills is found only in an old calaboose which appropriately sets the boundaries of their moral torpor and encloses them in a prison from which there is no escape. On the shores of Papeete, the "three most miserable English-speaking creatures in Tahiti" form an alliance based on misery and maintained by deceit. Each of the three—Herrick, Davis, and Huish—is an idler, and each has chosen the role of outcast rather than face responsibility. Herrick is the most pitiful for he shirks a responsibility for which he has been admirably trained. Well bred and Oxford educated, he is little more than a wastrel who attempts to retire to a world which will cater to his intellectual deficiency and his moral cowardice. He comes to the South Seas not out of choice but out of despair; retreating from trials he could not endure, he seeks to lose himself in an assumed name and an alien society. As he later confesses to Attwater, he is a "puppy," and his only possible action is to grovel before a strength he would like to possess and plead for a dissolution which he himself is too cowardly to perform.

Davis and Huish are Herrick's partners in misery. Davis is a dishonored sea captain whose weakness for drink has caused the loss of both his ship and his sailing papers. Still given to ranting upon his past actions, he can do little more than hope to drown them in a drunken forgetfulness. Like Herrick, he is a man with an eternal past which he cannot escape. Huish, on the other hand, is free from such restraints. Existing totally by and for himself, he is a man without an identity, for he has had so many that even he has difficulty distinguishing his true name from his aliases. A vagrant, he is free to live anywhere for his home is nowhere; thoroughly abandoned, he is capable of performing any action so long as it pleases his fancy. Existing on the edge of society, he is Stevenson's most chilling portrait of a raw egotism which has no other loyalty but to itself. Herrick, Davis, and Huish are suitable comrades since they personify the lowest ebb to which a man can sink—when he allows futility to become his passion and despair his ideal.

The first part of the novel details as gloomy a view of human existence as Stevenson claimed in his letters. Unwilling to foreclose all possibility of change so early in the narrative, however, he dangles the carrot of expectation for a while only to reveal finally that the rabbit run is a maze. The three desperados are given a chance at redemption by assuming command of an abandoned ship which they are supposed to deliver to its intended port. Characteristically, they choose instead to abscond with its cargo. No more successful at barratry than they had been in their other endeavors, they run aground upon an uncharted island and are forced to recognize their final failure as conclusive. Their destined "New Island" turns out to be a mockery of the New Jerusalem, for they find there condemnation, not salvation. Faced with submission to Attwater's "Last Judgment," Huish dies attempting to toss vitriol in his face; Davis chooses to be his "pet penitent"; and Herrick, after succumbing to his brutality, makes gestures at possibly returning to his home.

If the first part of the novel is grim, the second part is positively sinister. The New Island over which Attwater rules presents a vivid picture of a man-made hell, including its Satanic demagogue, its afflicted population, and its totally material concerns. What is more, this hell purports to be a heaven; for its rewards have been lucrative and its spiritual doctrine is ostensibly based upon Christian values. In a novel in which failure is the common experience, Attwater looms as the model of the self-made man: educated at Cambridge, confident to an inordinate degree, handsomely built, and imperiously aristocratic, he radiates success with all the vitality which clearly marks the other three as degenerate men. Having spent ten years on his island retreat, he has cultivated a flourishing pearl trade; and he becomes wealthy enough not only to live comfortably but to attempt to forge a new society. In doing so, he fancies himself an incarnation of the Christian God devoid of mercy, whose anger is in his glaring eye and whose justice is in his smiting hand. Dismissing conventional Christianity as womanish, he sets himself up as "a judge in Israel, the bearer of the sword and scourge."

Rather than God, Attwater is perversion incarnate; and his doctrine is a crude parody of Christian values: Christianity without Christ; justice without grace. The essence of his posture is his "silken brutality" with which he controls a native population and a regenerate pietist. Attwater looms in his frightening splendor as Stevenson's last testament to skepticism. Capable of maintaining a spiritual unity which had long been both a Victorian and Stevensonian ideal, Attwater's willful triumph is to trample upon his fellow creatures with all the dedication of a Carlylean hero turned Fascist. Cruel, insensible, uncompromising in the pursuit of his own interests, possessing manners without humanity—the words are all Herrick's—he represents the apex and nadir of civilization: the luminous ideal darkened by its own potential, a figure of elemental perversity turning upon itself and devouring its own flesh. Isolated upon a ravaged island, he commands the simple, the weak, and the morally infirm.

For all its power, however, *The Ebb-Tide* proves as disquieting as Stevenson's other fiction. Even here he cannot bring himself to utter the final words, to hurl idealism down "the void abysm" until it is "dragged captive through the deep." Thus at the end of the novel he includes a veiled hint that Herrick may leave Attwater's domain to face his responsibilities. The hint is characteristically oblique because Stevenson can neither affirm his faith in Herrick's return nor deny its possibility. The door is still left at least partially open, and so it remains. The two novels which follow are fragments; therefore, *The Ebb-Tide* represents what Stevenson first thought it to be, a "boss tract" which contains his closing, if not final, sermon.

CHAPTER 8

Requiem

WRITING under the influence of the 1920's, George S. Hellman entitled his biography of Stevenson, *The True Stevenson: A Study in Clarification* (1925). But, as in the popular game, the true Stevenson has yet to come forward. To his contemporaries, he was the sailor who set sail into the unknown, the darling of the armchair traveler who followed his adventures with avidity. To his friends, he was the unfortunate victim of health and household, never able to return to their masculine camaraderie. To his readers, he was the author of popular tales, the creator of John Silver, David Balfour, and Edward Hyde. Even he had difficulty defining himself. As versatile a writer as any in the century, he succeeded only occasionally in achieving his intentions; a creator of memorable villains, he brooded upon the gloomy cast of his literature and wished instead to be remembered as one who met life cheerfully. He chose his poem "Requiem" as his epitaph so that future generations would believe that its words summed up his life: "Glad did I live and gladly die."

But, as he well knew, the creative process is mysterious, and what emerges from the labyrinth of possibilities is often uncontrollable. The author in pursuit of nightingales may instead produce gothic gnomes. Henley touched on some of Stevenson's contradictions in his poem "Apparition," and Stevenson himself found "the war in the members" so much a part of his being that he considered it a universal law. Conflict is as much a part of his literature as his life; the conflict of man with man, with the universe, and most of all with himself. All of his protagonists must contend with forces both internal and external in a battle where failure is the only predictable result. Heroism is found not in victory but in resistance to inevitable defeat.

As conflict is a necessary ingredient in Stevenson's writing, it is likewise a necessary condition with which to evaluate that writing. All of his literature must be considered as the product of a constant struggle to maintain his intentions; a battle fought sometimes with his collaborator, often with an unyielding form, and always with a self-identity whose "secret shadows" emerged with perplexing regularity. The result, if mixed, is nonetheless memorable. In each genre, something of distinction remains, and as a master of narrative technique particularly Stevenson has few equals. Walter Allen in *The English Novel* (1954) suggests that Stevenson's "distinctive contribution to the English novel is that he successfully married Flaubert to Dumas. . . . His rediscovery of the art of narrative, of conscious and cunning calculation in telling a story so that the maximum effect of clarity and suspense is achieved, meant the birth of the novel of action as we know it, and the measure of the work of later writers such as John Buchan and Graham Greene . . ." (p. 336).

Stevenson's contribution to English literature is beginning to be understood by others as well. Recent bibliographies of Victorian literature suggest that he has begun to find favor among the academics. Too long confined to the nursery and the collector's shelf, his stories are now read and studied along with those of James, Meredith, and Conrad. Qualitative differences exist in each writer, and Stevenson would be the first to acknowledge them, but he would also wish to point out the quantitative distinctions. Essentially romances, Stevenson's fiction set out to explore man's ability to meet brute circumstance with little more than his natural instincts, in narratives which were necessarily opposed to particularity. A Stevenson narrative thrusts its characters directly into experience and challenges them to act with frightening immediacy. As they descend into the maelstrom, they testify to the contrarieties of God's world, and acknowledge that the lamb and the tiger were born of one Creator.

Notes and References

Chapter One

1. The best of Stevenson's biographers, J. C. Furnas, *Voyage to Windward* (New York, 1951), p. 207, cites an unpublished letter in which Stevenson facetiously instructs Henley to write a blackguard supplement to what he knows will be a respectable and thus false account of his life. He appropriately terms it "a masterpiece of the genteely evasive."

2. Henley's "blackguard supplement" appeared in the *Pall Mall Magazine* (December, 1901), 505–14, as a review of Balfour's *Life*. Despite his characteristic petulance, he at least partially restores Stevenson's identity. By 1901, Henley was sufficiently estranged from the Stevenson circle to counter its distortions with impunity. Unfortunately, he was not sufficiently distant from his own wounds for which he blamed not only Fanny but Stevenson. Too willing to reopen those wounds, Henley allowed his grievances to color his observations so that his distortions and those he attempted to clarify are often indistinguishable.

3. All references to Stevenson's works, except the poetry, are to the South Seas edition, 32 vols. (New York, 1925).

4. In an unpublished letter to Henley written at approximately the same time as the essay (Edinburgh City Library), Stevenson indicates that he regrets only that his father did not receive his deserved knighthood. The regret, however, is more bitter than sad. In fact, the entire letter suggests the painful distance of their relationship as Stevenson watched his father deteriorate into a stumbling caricature of his former, vigorous self. Unable to reach Edinburgh to see his father before death, his ill health prevented him from even attending the funeral, and he had to remain alone in the old house that he was no longer able to call home.

5. All references to Stevenson's poetry are to Janet Adams Smith, ed., *Robert Louis Stevenson: Collected Poems* (London, 1950). In this poem (p. 79), he pictures the light-keeper imprisoned not only within his tower but within his occupation. Unstirred by the life about him,

he gives up all "that is lovely in living/ For the means to live." Praised by many, he is revealed as a "martyr to a salary."

6. Furnas suggest that their domestic difficulties must have been severe, "for the Victorian wife did not lightly leave her husband" (p. 75).

7. DeLancey Ferguson and Marshall Waingrow, eds., *R.L.S.: Stevenson's Letters to Charles Baxter* (New Haven, 1956), p. 49. Until the complete letters are published, these remain the most authoritative.

8. One of the more significant discoveries of recent years is Bradford Booth's affirmation of Katherine Osbourne's charges against Stevenson's heirs. In the suppressed version of her book (*Robert Louis Stevenson in California* [Chicago, 1911]), Lloyd's first wife claimed that Fanny had a severe nervous breakdown during Stevenson's final years, and that she and her children were such financial drains that Stevenson forced himself to write at much cost to his health so that he could support a luxury that often strayed into immorality. As Booth began literally to uncover Stevenson's letters, to remove the strips of paper which Colvin had placed over words and passages, he discovered that Katherine's charges were not simply the whim of a wronged woman.

Booth summed up his tentative findings in an article written shortly before his death: "The long self-exile of Robert Louis Stevenson provided a romantic glow to his career, and the partial restoration of health and consequent mobility which he found in Samoa may well have added a few years to his life. But the costs in spirit were heavy. Isolated from his literary and artistic friends, nagged by a sense of creeping estrangement, nervous over the collapse of his wife, and wearied by the misbehavior of his numerous dependents, Stevenson did not find Vailima a haven of rest and peace." ("The Vailima Letters of Robert Louis Stevenson," *Harvard Library Bulletin* XV, 2 [April, 1967], 117–28).

9. The full poem is entitled "Apparition" and is part of Henley's *In Hospital* volume celebrating their first meeting. (*The Works of W. E. Henley*, I [London, 1908], p. 40).

10. After he had agreed to relinquish his interest in Stevenson's biography, Colvin became the editor of his letters. Before his death, Stevenson had written Baxter hoping to prevent such an occurrence because he knew that Colvin was not the person to make them public (Baxter letters, 322). Unfortunately, his suspicions were correct. Colvin published the letters only after he had carefully removed what he considered offensive and imposed his own personality on the Stevenson that emerges. His version is as much a fabrication as Balfour's.

Notes and References

Chapter Two

1. The essays are so used even by the most recent critics of Stevenson's fiction, Robert Kiely (*Robert Louis Stevenson and the Fiction of Adventure* [Cambridge, Mass.], 1964) and Edwin Eigner (*Robert Louis Stevenson and Romantic Tradition* [Princeton, 1966]). One critic who does not use them in this way, and whose chapter on the essays is a fine analysis of their style and structure, is David Daiches (*Robert Louis Stevenson* [Norwalk, Connecticut; 1947], pp. 148–72).

2. In Stevenson's essay "A College Magazine," he described his literary method with a phrase which has now become a cliché of Stevenson criticism: "Whenever I read a book or a passage that particularly pleased me . . . I must sit down at once and set myself to ape the quality. . . . I have thus played the sedulous ape to Hazlitt, to Lamb, to Wordsworth, to Sir Thomas Browne, to Defoe, to Hawthorne, to Montaigne, to Baudelaire, and to Obermann" (XIII, p. 35).

3. Not only does Stevenson mention Hazlitt first among those to whom he pays literary homage, but he was early engaged upon a life of his prose mentor which, like so many of his projects, never went beyond projection. Hazlitt represented much of that active vigor, both in his life and in his prose, that Stevenson longed to have.

4. Alice D. Snyder, "Paradox and Antithesis in Stevenson's Essays: A Structural Study," *Journal of English and Germanic Philology*, XIX, 4, (October, 1920), 540–59; Edward Snyder, "Another 'Apology for Idlers' in the Light of Some New Stevenson Discoveries," *Saturday Review of Literature* (August 3, 1935), p. 11; Jerome Hamilton Buckley, *William Ernest Henley: A Study in the "Counter-Decadence" of the 'Nineties'* (Princeton, 1945), p. 107; Edwin Eigner, "The Double in the Fiction of R. L. Stevenson," unpublished doctoral dissertation, State University of Iowa, 1963, p. 23.

5. Stevenson follows Hazlitt in attributing these lines which he quotes in *The Amateur Emigrant* and again in *An Inland Voyage* to "the old poet." James Hart, in his edition of Stevenson's American writings (*Robert Louis Stevenson: From Scotland to Silverado* [Cambridge, Mass., 1966], p. 72), speculates that Stevenson himself may have written the lines, but Hazlitt's earlier quotation in his essay "On Going a Journey" makes this impossible. The Wordsworth quotation which follows is of course from *The Prelude*, III, 195.

6. In one of his classic outbursts of loneliness, he writes to Mrs. Sitwell, of his three desiderata:

1. Good health
2. 2 to 3 hundred a year
3. O du lieber Gott, *friends*

(Letters, I, 216)

7. McClure, the American publisher, and the model of Jim Pinkerton in *The Wrecker*, had for some time been after Stevenson to write an account of a cruise which he would finance. At first reluctant to accept the lavish sum that McClure promised, Stevenson finally agreed to accept $10,000 to write a series of fifty "letters" about his voyage in the South Seas. However, after completing slightly more than half, Stevenson grew weary of presenting his impressions in this disconnected way and hoped instead to write a more artistic book. As he wearied, so too did his public and he soon abandoned the project for other work. The first twenty-five letters were published in the Edinburgh Edition after his death.

8. Stevenson had imagined himself a Ulysses in his poem "Youth and Love": "Hail and farewell! I must arise,/ Leave here the fatted cattle,/ And paint on foreign lands and skies/ My Odyssey of battle" (Smith, p. 246). Again in *Kidnapped* (see Chapter VII), he structures David's adventures so that they resemble the epic wanderings of the *Odyssey*. As he enacts the role, however, he carries his suggestions (and Tennyson's) into the void of Victorian skepticism. His Ulysses is finally most like Dante's, overwhelmed by a world whose dangers he could not help challenging.

9. In 1888, Stevenson wrote lyrics to the old tune of "Wandering Willie," and then incorporated some of them into the final pages of *The Master of Ballantrae*, just before the Master leaves his homeland forever. As a cry from his own exile, they are perhaps a more appropriate requiem than the one he wrote earlier, for they indicate that the sailor can never return from the sea nor the hunter from the hill (Smith, pp. 130, 256).

Chapter Three

1. Lloyd Osbourne's preface to the plays recreates some of the excitement that Henley generated with his scheme for writing plays that would insure riches: "R.L.S. was no longer to plod along as he had been doing; Henley was to abandon his grinding and ill-paid editorship; together they were to combine to write plays—marvellous plays that would run for hundreds of nights and bring in thousands of pounds. . . . R.L.S. entered enthusiastically into this collaboration, though, with his underlying Scotch caution, I doubt if he ever allowed himself to be wholly transported into Henley's fairyland. But he was stirred, nevertheless; shared to some degree, though reservedly, those ardent day-dreams of wealth; worked at the plays with extraordinary gusto and industry" (Plays, X, p. ix). Lloyd was right about Stevenson's caution. The pressures of writing were always wearying for him and those of playwrighting in particular. Writing to Henley in 1885, he indicates that his frustrations with the drama were severe

enough to dampen his enthusiasm for *Kidnapped,* a novel which he thought among his best: "I have thought as well as I could of what you said; and I have come unhesitatingly to the opinion that the stage is only a lottery, must not be regarded as a trade, and must never be preferred to drudgery. If money comes from any play, let us regard it as a legacy, but never count upon it in our income for the year. In other words, I must go on and drudge at *Kidnapped,* which I hate, and am unfit to do; and you will have to get some journalism somehow" (Letters, II, p. 254).

2. Furnas's rejection (p. 248) is somewhat understandable as that of a comprehensive biographer who wishes to go on to more substantial work, but Fanny's dismissal can only be seen as a transparent attempt to exonerate herself from any part in the plays' failure. In her preface to the *Jekyll and Hyde* volume (X), she places the burden totally upon Henley and blames his infectious enthusiasm for seducing both her and Stevenson into believing that the plays would lead to financial success. She pictures herself as an unwilling victim of Henley's persuasiveness when actually, as her unpublished letters show, she was at least partially responsible for stirring the fire of the supposedly lucrative venture. It is also indicative that she and Stevenson collaborated on a play, *The Hanging Judge,* after the failing of his collaboration with Henley.

3. Sir Arthur Wing Pinero, the British playwright, in an address before the Edinburgh Philosophical Institution, February 24, 1903, (reprinted as *Robert Louis Stevenson as a Dramatist, Columbia University Papers on Playmaking,* First Series, IV [New York, 1914]), indicts Stevenson and Henley for keeping their eye too set on gold and not enough upon the requirements of the drama. Frank Swinnerton, on the other hand (*Robert Louis Stevenson: A Critical Study* [New York, 1923], p. 94), accuses Stevenson of being a novelist who never understood that the drama demands other types of responses than the novel. Swinnerton singles out Stevenson's lack of "the visual sense," yet few novelists are as visual and his plays can hardly be considered static representations. In fact, part of Stevenson's difficulty was to mute the cruder visual effects in order to create greater depth in his characters. He failed despite his awareness of what the drama demanded.

4. Harriet Dorothea Macpherson, *R.L. Stevenson: A Study in French Influence* (New York, 1930), p. 13, claims that Stevenson was fascinated by the French drama and that, while in Paris, he regularly went to the theater.

5. Skelt and Pollock were the two entrepreneurs of the cardboard theaters that so fascinated Stevenson as a child and whom he celebrated in the essay, "A Penny Plain and Twopence Coloured." His

later dramatic experience is discussed by Graham Balfour (p. 135): "The theatre was a great delight to him. Although he had read (and written) plays from his early years, had revelled in the melodrama of the toy-theatre, and had acted with the Jenkins and in other private theatricals, I find no record of his having visited a theatre before December 1874 when he found Irving's Hamlet 'interesting (for it is really studied) but not good,' and there is no sign of his having been really impressed until he saw Salvini as Macbeth at Edinburgh in the spring of 1876."

6. Letter quoted by E. V. Lucas, *The Colvins and their Friends* (London, 1928), p. 108. Lucas dates it June 20, 1879. In his essay on Alexandre Dumas, *Views and Reviews,* I, 42, Henley repeats similar ideas toward drama: "Drama to him was so much emotion in action. If he invented a situation he accepted its issues in their entirety, and did his utmost to express from it all the passion it contained."

7. There remain unpublished a number of letters from Stevenson to Henley concerning their projected aims and ensuing difficulties in relation to the drama. Many of these are in the Edinburgh City Library. While in Edinburgh I had the opportunity to examine them and found hitherto little known information on the strains of collaboration. Complementary letters from Henley to Stevenson in the Beinecke Library complete what amounts to a vivid account of a troubled partnership and help to explain the tensions which made the "Quarrel Letters" inevitable.

8. Eric Bentley, *The Life of the Drama* (New York, 1964), p. 217: "Melodrama . . . is drama in its elemental form; it is the quintessence of drama. The impulse to write drama is, in the first instance, the impulse to write melodrama. . . ."

9. Henley's catalogue of projected plays which he incorporated into his review of Graham Balfour's biography is a sad record of unaccomplishment. Those he mentions, and those listed by Balfour (p. 220), rest upon the ruins of a promising relationship which weathered all storms but the last.

10. Those who blame Henley for being so caught up in the promised success of the plays that he was insensitive to the growing disparity between himself and Stevenson should consider his letter to Charles Baxter, written shortly after the London failure of *Deacon Brodie* (July 1884): "We (Louis and I) have talked the thing over—reconstruction and all; & I can see my way to making a play of it. But frankly, I don't expect we shall ever get to work on the thing again; nor for that matter on anything else. The match is no longer equal. Louis has grown faster than I have . . ." (Beinecke Library 4610).

11. As the unpublished letters make clear, Stevenson and Henley

worked so closely on the plays that any attempt to separate their responsibilities is futile. Stevenson, in fact, at least once attempted to quiet such speculation. Responding to the editor of *The Epoch*, he corrected the hypothesis that Henley had little to do with the writing of *Brodie* and assured him that there is no line in the whole play that does not represent the work of both authors. Yet the letters also indicate that despite Stevenson's protestations, each of the plays reveals an identifiable influence.

12. The comparison is made by Jerome Hamilton Buckley, *William Henley*, p. 108.

13. A copy of the first version of *Brodie* is in the Beinecke Library. It has also been printed in the Monterey Edition of Stevenson's works (New York, 1906), Vol. VIII.

14. Henley to Stevenson, April 20, 1880 (Beinecke Library 4736): "Warner is fascinated by the part—fascinated, eaten up, overcome with it, but he does not love it. He is a good man, & to be in love with the Deacon he would have to be as wicked as Frédérick. He would play it, and with a mighty joy; but he would feel a martyr in it too. The public could not sympathise with him, and sympathise the public must, or the play goes to hell."

15. In two unpublished letters to Henley from Hyères (March, 1883?), Stevenson dictates the changes necessary to make *Brodie* the kind of play he wants it to be. His first consideration is that the play end absolutely in the reverse key and that every detail lead up to this reversal. Accordingly, Brodie's death must be softened, and he must die with only a silent hope of redemption.

16. Bentley, pp. 241, 255: "Farce brings together the direct and wild fantasies and the everyday and drab realities. The interplay between the two is the very essence of this art—the farcical dialectic. If we go on to speak of a contrast in farce between mask and face, symbol and thing symbolized, appearance and reality, this will not be a contrast in styles but a contrast between either the gravity or the gaiety on the surface and whatever lies beneath. . . . Melodrama and farce are both arts of escape and what they are running away from is not only social problems but all other forms of moral responsibility."

17. In his essay, "Reflections and Remarks on Human Life," (II, p. 221), Stevenson clearly distinguishes between selfishness and egoism: "Selfishness is calm, a force of nature: you might say the trees were selfish. But egoism is a piece of vanity; it must always take you into its confidence; it is uneasy, troublesome, seeking; it can do good, but not handsomely; it is uglier, because less dignified, than selfishness itself."

18. For an account of Newton's life, see Bernard Martin, *Ancient Mariner* (New York, 1960).

19. Meredith's letter was partially published by the Anderson Galleries in their catalogue advertising the sale of Stevenson MSS. It is dated October 15, 1884. *Autograph Letters, Original Manuscripts, . . . from the Library of Robert Louis Stevenson,* Sold at the Anderson Galleries, November 23–25, 1914, p. 69.

20. Beinecke Library 4768, July 14, 1883. Henley continues: "The Shakespeare of tomorrow will take for his hero, not Othello, but Iago. The heroes of iniquity, the epic of immorality, the drama of vice— voilà la vraie affaire. In fifty years the Deacon, if we had but done it, might be a great work. We are syphilised to the core, & we don't know it. Zola is our papular eruption, as Balzac was our primary sore. Presently, we shall get to our tertiaries; & the Ugly will be as the Beautiful. . . ."

21. Letters, II, p. 327. This letter is only one of several in which Stevenson remarks upon his reluctance to explore the complications of his fiction. A Romantic, he preferred a literature of bird-haunted pleasure but found himself unavoidably attracted to stories which were haunted by more sinister creatures.

Chapter Four

1. Both H. W. Garrod and Janet Adams Smith accept Stevenson's self-estimation as only partially valid. For Garrod in his two essays on Stevenson's poetry, "The Poetry of R. L. Stevenson," *The Profession of Poetry* (Oxford, 1929), pp. 179–93, and "The Poetry of R. L. Stevenson," *Essays Mainly on the Nineteenth Century Presented to Sir Humphrey Milford* (Oxford, 1949), pp. 42–57, Stevenson's prosaic quality is often balanced by a lyric sweetness, while Miss Smith describes Stevenson in her introduction as "a master of the occasional poem."

2. Garrod begins his later essay with a citation from the numerous instances in which Stevenson disparaged his poetic efforts. In citing these, Garrod quite rightly views them suspiciously as a protest by a prose artist wary of calling undue attention to his poetic inferiority. One should always remember that despite his protests Stevenson never stopped writing poetry and that he allowed several volumes of his verse to be published. In contrast to his abortive career as a dramatist, he continued to write poetry until his death.

3. Stevenson's imitative powers in poetry were indeed as immense as his prose talents, or so it would seem from the diverse influences which Garrod and Smith see upon his verse. The first looks to Arnold and Swinburne; the second invokes the shades of Horace, Martial, and Herrick.

4. The modern Scots poets' debt to Stevenson has been analyzed by Kurt Wittig, *The Scottish Tradition in Literature* (Edinburgh, 1958),

p. 275, and with greater precision by James Kinsley, *Scottish Poetry: A Critical Survey* (London, 1955), p. 247. They both indicate that, with an irony which Stevenson would have appreciated, his influence upon them has been greater than upon the prose writers. Certainly no native novelist can point to him with quite as much assurance as can MacDiarmid and Sydney Goodsir Smith.

5. Three volumes of poems were published in Stevenson's lifetime: *A Child's Garden of Verses* (1885), *Underwoods* (1887), and *Ballads* (1890). *Songs of Travel* was prepared by Stevenson but seen through the press by Colvin and first published in the Edinburgh Edition, 1895. In 1914, shortly after her mother's death, Isobel Strong placed on sale at the Anderson Galleries in New York many of her stepfather's manuscript notebooks, several of which contained unpublished poems. After this sale, some new poems crept in to the official editions while others were published in separate volumes or as part of "revelatory" biographies.

6. As fine as her collection is, Miss Smith occasionally betrays the difficulty of classification. She considers some poems as comic, yet there is often little to distinguish between poems in this category and those placed elsewhere. Her rationale seems to be that poems in this section are less important than others (p. 53), yet it is difficult to know what to consider important. For example, No. III, contained in a letter to Charles Baxter, is a fine statement of the Stevenson doctrine of idleness, while No. IV, "Ne Sit Ancillae Tibi Pudori," seemed important enough to George Hellman to claim that Stevenson was having an affair with his housekeeper. Not wishing to quibble over definitions, I have chosen to call comic all verse that is intentionally and actually humorous.

7. Again Miss Smith creates some confusion by classifying these as poems for children. J. C. Furnas (p. 203) rightly considers them as comic poetry and distinguishes between a childish abandon which Stevenson presumably never possessed and the childlike play which pervades the poetry with a worldly-wise laughter.

8. The Davos press was the miniature printing press which Lloyd brought with him to Davos from California. At first he alone amused himself with it by printing doggerel and mock adventure stories, but then Stevenson joined in and supplied both woodcuts and text.

9. In an unpublished letter to Henley in the Edinburgh City Library, Stevenson writes that the ballad he has just completed is "a genteel muddle of Lord Macaulay and the old ones."

10. Stevenson to Colvin, June, 1884 (Letters, II, p. 201): "As soon as I have all the slips I shall organise the book for the publisher. A set of 8 will be put together under the title *An Only Child;* another cycle of 10 will be called *In the Garden,* and the other six called

Bedtime to end all up. It will now make quite a little volume of a good way upwards of 100 pp." Although the names changed and the size of the volume increased, the order remained an integral necessity to the success of the poems. After he determined the final sequence, Stevenson wrote again to Colvin: "I never knew anything cost me so much actual *pain* as this morsel of rearrangement." (quoted in Smith, p. 48).

11. In a note to the Scots poems in *Underwoods*, Stevenson explains his method: "I simply wrote my Scots as well as I was able, not caring if it hailed from Lauderdale or Angus, from the Mearns or Galloway; if I had ever heard a good word, I used it without shame. . . . And if it be not pure, alas! what matters it?" The modern Scots poets have followed Stevenson's lead in making their vernacular a synthesis of local dialects.

12. An interesting comment on Scott's use of native speech may be found in David Craig, *Scottish Literature and the Scottish People 1680–1830* (London, 1961), pp. 254–58. Craig points out that Scott in effect creates two languages, a conventional English prose with which he is never fully comfortable but which he uses because it is the accepted language, and a native Scots which he handles freely but with marked embarrassment.

13. As he became increasingly burdened by his sense of separation, Stevenson increasingly emphasized his kinship with Fergusson and Burns, raising his association with the former particularly to the level of psychic identity. Looking back upon his life, he found special meaning as the descendant of Edinburgh's gifted boy who died young, neglected by his native city. Although Edinburgh now pays partial homage to Fergusson by attending his grave, that city of many monuments has none to honor Stevenson, whom it still chooses to neglect.

Chapter Five

1. In her unpublished doctoral dissertation, Margaret Cecilia Annan ("*The Arabian Nights* in Victorian Literature," Northwestern University, 1945) reviews the contemporary reactions to the tales, and her citations suggest that the nineteenth-century critic knew as little of Stevenson's intentions as his twentieth-century counterpart. For the most part, the tales have considered as youthful pranks with as much substance as those cream tarts which the gay young man in the first story swallows with such abandon. The value of Miss Annan's study is twofold: she understands Stevenson's parodic intent, and she places the stories in their *Arabian Nights* context.

2. In her discussion, Miss Annan emphasizes that Stevenson's love of the original tales was prompted by an awareness of their comic versatility, which he made a necessary condition of his achievement.

Notes and References

3. Amy Cruse, *The Victorians and their Reading* (Boston, 1936), pp. 286, 291, includes *The Arabian Nights* as a standard component of every young Victorian's library and claims it was often retained on the shelf even in adulthood. Certainly this was true later in the century with Burton's and Payne's translations. The one-time child's classic had suddenly grown into a work of erotic notoriety. Even in the older versions, however, there were few writers of the century that were not influenced by it.

4. Margaret Annan devotes a major portion of her discussion of Stevenson's tales (pp. 343–56) to an attempt to prove that Prince Florizel is an obvious satire on the Prince of Wales and his love of playful disguise. Stevenson may very well have had a living model in mind for Prince Florizel, yet even without the Prince of Wales he had a given literary example in Haroun Al Raschid, the wayward monarch of the traditional tales to whom role-playing is a way of life.

5. In her introduction to *The Dynamiter* volume, Fanny indicates that the inspiration for the stories came from "several dynamite outrages in London about this time, the most of them turning out fiascos." She also claims that the stories are mainly hers. One of several unresolved questions in Stevenson studies is exactly this question of collaboration.

The correspondence with Henley helps somewhat to clarify the nature of their literary relationship, but Stevenson's partnership with Lloyd and Fanny still remains a mystery. There are fragmentary accounts in relation to particular works sufficient to suggest that in almost every case Stevenson finished what was begun by his partner, and I have followed their suggestions in discussing the collaborative fiction.

6. Letters, II, 246 (to John Addington Symonds, February, 1885): "We believe in nothing, Symonds: you don't and I don't; and there are two reasons, out of a handful of millions, why England stands before the world dripping with blood and daubed with dishonour. . . . See, for example, if England has shown . . . one spark of manly sensitivity, they have been shamed into it by the spectacle of Gordon. Police-Officer Cole is the only man that I see to admire. I dedicate my *New Arabs* to him and Cox, in default of other great public characters."

7. Alexander Reid, "R. L. S.—A Psychological Novelist?," *Scotland's Magazine* (January, 1960), pp. 55–56, sees the recurring metaphor in Stevenson's fiction as a search for hidden treasure.

8. Stevenson's somewhat comic term for atavism in several of his essays. In "The Manse," he imagines his clergyman-grandfather as sitting in his study unaware of his link with the past: "as he sat in his

cool study, grave, reverend, contented gentleman, there was an aboriginal frisking of the blood that was not his; tree-top memories, like
undeveloped negatives, lay dormant in his mind; tree-top instincts
awoke and were trod down; and Probably Arboreal (scarce to be
distinguished from a monkey) gambolled and chattered in the brain
of the old divine" (XIII, 65). Again, in "Pastoral," he speaks of "a
certain low-browed, hairy gentleman, at first a percher in the fork
of trees, next (as they relate) a dweller in caves . . . his name I never
heard, but he is often described as Probably Arboreal, which may serve
for recognition" (XIII, 57).

9. Ann Gossman, "On The Knocking At the Gate in 'Markheim',"
Nineteenth-Century Fiction, XVII (June, 1962), 73–76; Joseph J.
Egan, " 'Markheim': A drama of Moral Psychology," *Nineteenth-Cen-
tury Fiction*, XX (March, 1966), 377–84.

10. Edgar C. Knowlton, "A Russian Influence on Stevenson," *Modern Philology*, XIV (December, 1916). 449, considers "Markheim" to
be a cameo version of *Crime and Punishment*.

11. The best catalogue—and it is little more than that—of the
Doppelganger tradition is Ralph Tymms's, *Doubles in Literary Psychology* (Cambridge, Eng., 1949). His inability to produce more
than an extensive list of the Doppelganger's appearance indicates both
the widespread nature of its influence as well as the difficulty of distinguishing between its several forms. For a more satisfying study
see Masao Miyoshi, *The Divided Self* (New York, 1969). Numerous
critics have commented on Nabokov's indebtedness to the tradition,
so much so, that in a recent interview, *Nabokov: The Man and His
Work*, ed. L. S. Dembo (Madison, Wisc., 1967), pp. 19–44, he dismisses the subject as "a frightful bore."

12. James Baird, *Ishmael: A Study of the Symbolic Mode in Primitivism* (New York, 1960), p. 138: "Of the artists here related to the
Pacific and the Orient, he is the one least disturbed by his Protestant
inheritance. In fact, he is another Ishmael scarcely at all, but a man
sensitive to every new experience and remarkably curious about its
potentiality *as narrative*."

13. The copy I consulted is in the Huntington Library. In this
tract "written for fun," Stevenson uses John Wiltshire as his spokesman against the authoritarian regulations which the British Govern-
ment attempted to enforce upon the Samoans.

Chapter Six

1. In Paul Willstach, *Richard Mansfield: The Man and the Actor*
(New York, 1909), facing p. 146. Mansfield played Hyde as a manifestation of Jekyll's lust, a creature of infinite sexual drive who "unable by reason of his hideous shape to indulge the dreams of his

hideous imagination," proceeds to satisfy his cravings in violence (quoted from Mansfield's notes in the Huntington Library).

The transfer from stage to screen only confirmed Mansfield's interpretation. John Barrymore (1920) played Hyde as the essence of a lust-ridden fiend, eyeing his victims with rapacious lubricity. A latter-day Dorian Gray, he is more Oscar Wilde's man than Stevenson's and his pleasure-seeking forays into the shadowy world of Soho are clearly echoes from Wilde's novel. Rouben Mamoulian's 1932 version with Frederic March in the dual role increased the sexual overtones. Not content with suggestive pleasure haunts, Mamoulian inserted the character of Ivy, the attractive barmaid whose charms so affect the pent-up Jekyll that he must indulge in sexual atrocities in order to satisfy his cravings. Later versions—1941, 1968—with Spencer Tracy and Jack Palance in the respective title roles followed the standard pattern with little ingenuity.

What emerges from all this is a portrait of Hyde with a decidedly modern veneer: released by the intemperate tastes of Jekyll, he exists in order to allow his double to gratify his wanton lusts. As Edwin Eigner remarks: "It is perhaps unfortunate . . . that all four of the important stage and screen productions of *Jekyll and Hyde* were made in America, where the popular mind is especially apt to regard sex and evil as synonymous terms" (p. 150).

2. Stevenson's attempts to convince people that Jekyll is pronounced with a long "e" (see Furnas, p. 304) may be ranked with his unsuccessful efforts to withstand Hyde's equation with sexuality.

3. See Masao Miyoshi, *The Divided Self* (New York, 1969). I am also indebted to Mr. Miyoshi for some suggestive ideas contained in his article "Dr. Jekyll and the Emergence of Mr. Hyde," *College English*, XXVII (March, 1966), 470–80.

4. Few critics have written so well—with both wit and clarity—about Stevenson as Chesterton. Yet here he tries too hard to make one point and thereby misses another. G. K. Chesterton, *Robert Louis Stevenson* (London, n.d.), pp. 68–69.

5. The narrative technique recalls Hogg's *The Private Memoirs and Confessions of a Justified Sinner*, with its opening "Editor's Narrative," and its subsequent confession by the Jekyll-like younger brother. Yet, as Lionel Stevenson suggests in a note, an eclectic writer like Stevenson might also have found his model in the novels of Wilkie Collins. Edwin Eigner, for example, discusses his indebtedness to *Frankenstein* (pp. 161–64), while the necessary integration of natural and social is of central concern in Meredith. Whatever his sources, Stevenson was able to use them well.

6. My impression of Victorian literature, although tentative, is that it grows increasingly internal. Not only are more novels set in cities,

but the action of those novels takes place within interior settings. The parallel phenomenon here is the increasing regularity of the box set and the simultaneous loss of the stage apron. The retreat behind a frame becomes a physical symbol for a social condition; the domestic melodrama becomes at once the popular vehicle and the cardinal metaphor, a synthesis of fantasy and reality.

7. Walter Houghton, *The Victorian Frame of Mind* (New Haven, 1957), p. 343.

8. Both Ian Watt, *The Rise of the Novel* (Berkeley, 1959), pp. 174–207, and Steven Marcus, *The Other Victorians* (New York, 1967), p. 250, provide discussions of privatization and its relationship to literature. Watt is particularly cogent on the course of modern literature, while Marcus draws special attention to pornography. What Marcus indicates is that the reading habits (not to speak of other practices) of underground man were often extensions of social behavior. As his reading habits represent "a further withdrawal into the arcane," so too the locations of the novels he read represent an increasing internalization. It is not surprising, for example, that so much of Victorian underground literature takes place indoors. The narrator of *A Man With A Maid* wishes to build a mechanical sexual paradise within the confines of his rented flat, while Walter, in *My Secret Life,* has intercourse with a workman's wife in the uninhabited building her husband just completed.

9. Despite some difference in details, all accounts of the writing of *Jekyll and Hyde* indicate that Fanny objected to its initial sensationalism and suggested that it be rewritten as an allegory. Though Isobel Strong indicates in an unpublished letter that Fanny actually helped with the revision, her suggestions alone clearly pointed the story in its successful direction.

10. Quoted by George S. Hellman, *The True Stevenson* (Boston, 1925), p. 129.

11. Stevenson's symbolic structure has led to speculation on the significance of Jekyll's and Hyde's name. A recent suggestion by Joseph J. Egan ("The Relationship of Theme and Art in *The Strange Case of Dr. Jekyll and Mr. Hyde," English Literature in Transition,* IX [1966], 28–32), is that Jekyll is from the French Je = self, and kyll = kill; in other words a designated self-destroyer. The speculation of Hyde's name has been less imaginative. Stevenson himself hints at a possible reading when he has Utterson say, "If he be Mr. Hyde, I shall be Mr. Seek." The reference is both to the children's game of pursuit and to the hidden being of that quest whose secret refuge must be discovered and revealed. In short, Mr. Hyde is very much "it." In addition, his name may be suggestive of another meaning of hide, one's external animality which serves as both assertion and pro-

tection. Yet, the multiple shadings in his name remain uncertain. In this regard, as in others, the richness of the story is a quality of its indefinite connotations.

12. An important indication that pre-Freudian analysis had already begun to distort the story may be taken from F. W. Myers's letters to Stevenson on *Jekyll and Hyde*. Myers was one of the founders of the Society for Psychical Research and, with the recommendation of Symonds, wrote to Stevenson shortly after the story's publication. Mistaking Stevenson's politeness for genuine interest (see letter to Myers, II, 294), he sent off five large sheets of comments upon specific details, many of which he wished corrected. A survey of these notes (now in the Beinecke Library) indicates that Myers chose to read the story as a realistic portrayal of specialized psychic phenomena. Accordingly, Myers asked that Jekyll's goodness be more apparent, that Hyde's crimes be more overtly sexual, and that all else be in keeping with the verities of psychological experimentation. Many of his readings are ingenious, yet he expends "much spirit in a waste of shame." In attempting to turn the story into a case study of psychical transference, he tramples upon its broader moral significance.

Chapter Seven

1. The corollary of romance is pornography, with its visions of unlimited possibility and its unadorned depictions of traditional stimuli which attempt to transform the verbal present into a pictorial eternity. A vivid example of their relationship may be found in that remarkable Victorian tale of sexual adventure, *The Romance of Lust*. Its hero, Charlie Roberts, pursues sexual excitement with all the gusto of a quest for gold. Indeed, as Steven Marcus points out, the lust for money and the lust for sexual pleasure are often related pursuits, arising as they do from a meeting of the individual will and a social ethos which values acquisition as one of its essential drives. Their kinship is driven home with an often crude directness throughout much of Victorian underground literature. *Treasure Island* likewise reduces material society to its basics but, of course, turns pornographic crudity into metaphor.

2. Furnas, p. 198: "He was pleased, of course, when Lang told him that, as romance, the book stood only below the *Odyssey* and *Tom Sawyer;* but to word that Mr. Gladstone, whom Louis detested, sat up all night to read it and was recommending it on all sides, Louis snapped back that the Grand Old Man 'would do better to attend to the imperial affairs of England.'"

3. This was Stevenson's term for precious hackwork, and it governed his opinion of *The Black Arrow* even after its book-length pub-

lication. Writing to William Archer in 1894, he complains: "It is an odd fact, or perhaps a very natural one; I find few greater pleasures than reading my own works, but I never, O I never read *The Black Arrow*" (Letters, IV, 269).

4. One of the most fascinating mysteries in the annals of Scottish history, the murder of Colin Campbell is still unsolved. Most authorities agree that an innocent man was hanged for the crime, and most also agree that Alan Breck was at most a confederate of the man who pulled the trigger.

5. Edwin Eigner's claim that Stevenson used *Huckleberry Finn* as his model for *Kidnapped* is questionable (pp. 79–82). Yet it is certain that Stevenson was impressed with Twain's novel and its appealing moral conflict. Shortly after reading it he writes to Symonds: "Have you read *Huckleberry Finn?* It contains many excellent things; above all, the whole story of a healthy boy's dealings with his conscience, incredibly well done" (Letters, II, 245).

6. Quiller-Couch's ending brings the action to its expected satisfactory conclusion but its language is so stale and its movement so static that it serves primarily to make the first part of the novel look that much better. Colvin's editorial note appended to all editions of *Weir*, though only suggestive, is usually looked upon as final authority since he claims to have received his information from Isobel Strong, to whom the novel was dictated. The events as Colvin outlines them are to conclude with Christina's seduction and pregnancy by Archie's former acquaintance, Frank Innes, Archie's slaying of Frank in a duel, his conviction before his father, his confinement in prison, and his eventual rescue by Christina's brothers. Since all agree that this ending is unsatisfactory perhaps Stevenson would have thought so as well. He frequently changed his novels as he wrote them and there is no certainty that he would have continued in this direction. *Weir of Hermiston*, both to its credit and to its detriment, remains unrealized and any attempt to write its conclusion can only be an exercise in conjecture.

7. In his essay, "The Genesis of *The Master of Ballantrae*," (XVIII, xxii), Stevenson indicates that the crush of events in their several locations was an intended part of the narrative structure. In addition, his letters written during the composition of the novel suggest the same precise planning. Stevenson always had difficulty with the long narrative since his intentions were best realized in sharp effect. The "failure" of *The Master*, however, is due not to its sagging strength (or Stevenson's) but to its overwhelmingly imposing action.

8. Letter to Colvin, Letters, IV, 299: "Your pleasing letter *re The Ebb-Tide*, to hand. I propose, if it be not too late, to delete Lloyd's

name. He has nothing to do with the last half. The first we wrote together, as the beginning of a long yarn. The second is entirely mine; and I think it rather unfair on the young man to couple his name with so infamous a work."

Selected Bibliography

PRIMARY SOURCES

1. *Collected Editions*
   None of the collected editions is more authoritative than another,
   but the later editions contain more material: poems, early essays,
   unfinished stories. I list the three that were most helpful to me:
   The Edinburgh Edition, 28 vols. London: Chatto and Windus,
   1894–1898. The first collected edition.
   Vailima Edition, 26 vols. London: Longmans, Green, Co., 1922–
   1923. The most elegant edition, incorporating the newly discovered poetry, The Hanging Judge, and other material left out of
   the earlier editions.
   South Seas Edition, 32 vols. New York: Scribners, 1925. The last
   of the collected editions and most complete on the letters.

2. *Collected Essays*
   The date in all cases is the date of first publication.
   An Inland Voyage. London: Kegan, Paul & Co., 1878.
   Picturesque Notes on Edinburgh. London: Seeley and Co., 1878.
   Travels With a Donkey in the Cevennes. London: Kegan, Paul & Co.,
   1879.
   Virginibus Puerisque. London: Kegan, Paul & Co., 1881.
   Familiar Studies of Men and Books: London: Chatto and Windus,
   1882.
   The Silverado Squatters. London: Chatto and Windus, 1883.
   Memories and Portraits. London: Chatto and Windus, 1887.
   The South Seas: A Record of Three Cruises. Edinburgh Edition, 1890.
   Across the Plains, with Other Memories and Essays. London: Chatto
   and Windus, 1892.
   A Footnote to History. London: Cassell & Co., 1892.

3. *Collected Poems*
   A Child's Garden of Verses. London: Longmans, Green & Co., 1885.
   Underwoods. London: Chatto and Windus, 1887.
   Ballads. London: Chatto and Windus, 1891.
   Songs of Travel. Edinburgh Edition, 1895.

4. Collected Stories

New Arabian Nights. London: Chatto and Windus, 1882.
More New Arabian Nights. London: Longmans, Green & Co., 1885.
The Merry Men. London: Chatto and Windus, 1887.
Islands Nights' Entertainments. London: Cassell & Co., 1893.

5. Novels

Treasure Island. London: Cassell & Co., 1883.
Prince Otto. London: Chatto and Windus, 1885.
Strange Case of Dr. Jekyll and Mr. Hyde. London: Longmans, Green & Co., 1886.
Kidnapped. London: Cassell & Co., 1886.
The Black Arrow. London: Cassell & Co., 1888.
The Master of Ballantrae. London: Cassell & Co., 1889.
The Wrecker. London: Cassell & Co., 1892.
Catriona. London: Cassell & Co., 1893.
The Ebb-Tide. London: Heinemann, 1894.
Weir of Hermiston. London: Chatto and Windus, 1896.
St. Ives. New York: Scribners, 1897.

SECONDARY SOURCES

1. Works Directly Related to Stevenson

Autograph Letters, Original Manuscripts, etc., from the Library of Robert Louis Stevenson. New York: Privately Printed, 1914. The sale catalogue of the first major sale of Stevenson material.

ANNAN, MARGARET CECILIA. "The Arabian Nights in Victorian Literature." Unpublished doctoral dissertation, Northwestern University, 1945. Especially valuable for Stevenson's use of the tales.

BALFOUR, GRAHAM. The Life of Robert Louis Stevenson. London: Methuen, 1915. Official biography.

BOOTH, BRADFORD A. "The Vailima Letters of Robert Louis Stevenson." Harvard Library Bulletin, XV, 28 (April, 1967), 117–28. Brief glimpse into the kind of disclosures that Booth's edition of the complete letters would have provided. With Booth's death, the publication of the letters remains uncertain.

BROWN, GEORGE E. A Book of R.L.S. London: Methuen, 1919. Handy guide to Stevenson details.

BUCKLEY, JEROME HAMILTON. William Ernest Henley: A Study in the "Counter-Decadence" of the 'Nineties.' Princeton: Princeton University Press, 1945. Informative study of Henley, Stevenson, their circle, and their times.

CHESTERTON, G. K. Robert Louis Stevenson. London: Hodder and Stoughton, n.d. Excellent early study; still remains among the best.

Selected Bibliography

CONNELL, JOHN. *W. E. Henley.* London: Constable, 1949. Somewhat more detailed; not so valuable as Buckley's study. Often inaccurate.

DAICHES, DAVID. *Robert Louis Stevenson.* Norwalk, Connecticut: New Directions, 1947. Model of gentlemanly criticism by the modern Chesterton.

————. *Stevenson and the Art of Fiction.* New York: Privately Printed, 1951. Address celebrating the Yale Library acquisition of the Beinecke Collection.

EGAN, JOSEPH J. "Artistic Design and the Ambiguities of Reality: Craft and Idea in the Fiction of Robert Louis Stevenson." Unpublished doctoral dissertation, Notre Dame University, 1965.

————. "The Relationship of Theme and Art in *The Strange Case of Dr. Jekyll and Mr. Hyde.*" *English Literature in Transition,* IX (1966), 28–32. Speculative article which makes some interesting suggestions.

————. "Markheim: A Drama of Moral Psychology," *Nineteenth-Century Fiction,* XX (March, 1966), 377–84. Better developed article which examines the symbolic structure of the story.

————. "From History to Myth: A Symbolic Reading of *The Master of Ballantrae.*" *Studies in English Literature,* VIII (1968), 699–710. Suggests that James and Henry are necessary complements of one another, as well as representatives of Jacobite and Whig.

————. "Dark in the Poet's Corner: Stevenson's 'A Lodging for the Night'." *Studies in Short Fiction,* VII (1970), 402–08. Considers Villon as a typical Stevenson villain because of his abandonment of decency.

EIGNER, EDWIN. "The Double in the Fiction of R. L. Stevenson." Unpublished doctoral dissertation, State University of Iowa, 1963.

————. *Robert Louis Stevenson and Romantic Tradition.* Princeton: Princeton University Press, 1966. Uneven book, too much a reworking of the dissertation. Intensive discussion of some often neglected works.

FERGUSON, DELANCEY and WAINGROW, MARSHALL. *R.L.S.: Stevenson's Letters to Charles Baxter.* New Haven: Yale University Press, 1956. Most authoritative edition of any letters to date.

FURNAS, J. C. *Voyage to Windward.* New York: William Sloane Associates, 1951. Best, most reliable biography. Contains some fine critical readings and an extensive bibliography.

GARROD, H. W. "The Poetry of R. L. Stevenson." *The Profession of Poetry.* Oxford: Oxford University Press, 1929. One of the earliest studies of Stevenson's poetry.

————. "The Poetry of R. L. Stevenson." *Essays Mainly on the Nineteenth Century Presented to Sir Humphrey Milford.* Oxford: Oxford University Press, 1948. More substantial study from which Stevenson emerges as a cross between Arnold and Housman.

GOSSMAN, ANN. "On the Knocking at the Gate in 'Markheim'." *Nineteenth-Century Fiction*, XVII (June, 1962), 73–76. Relationship between *Macbeth*, DeQuincey, and Stevenson.

GWYNN, STEPHEN. *Robert Louis Stevenson.* London: Macmillan, 1939. Some interesting though erratic readings.

HART, JAMES A. *Robert Louis Stevenson: From Scotland to Silverado.* Cambridge, Massachusetts: Harvard University Press, 1966. Excellent edition of Stevenson's writings about his travels in America.

HELLMAN, GEORGE S. *The True Stevenson: A Study in Clarification.* Boston: Little, Brown, 1925. Best of the debunking biographies.

HENLEY, WILLIAM ERNEST. *Collected Works.* London: D. Nutt, 1908.

———. "R.L.S." *The Pall Mall Magazine* (December, 1901), 505–514. Henley's acerbic review of Balfour's biography; contains his bitter memories of his former friend.

———. Unpublished letters to Robert Louis Stevenson. Beinecke Library. These letters complement Stevenson's on the dramatic collaboration.

KIELY, ROBERT. *Robert Louis Stevenson and the Fiction of Adventure.* Cambridge, Massachusetts: Harvard University Press, 1964. Generally sound reading of Stevenson's fiction; only somewhat limited by a Conradian perspective and a Freudian bias.

LUCAS, E. V. *The Colvins and their Friends.* London: Methuen, 1928. Contains vital information about the working relations between Colvin and his two "boys," Henley and Stevenson.

MACKAY, MARGARET. *The Violent Friend: The Story of Mrs. Robert Louis Stevenson.* New York: Doubleday, 1968. A recent biography of Fanny which, despite itself, cannot disguise some of her less attractive characteristics.

MANSFIELD, RICHARD. Unpublished notes to his interpretation of *Dr. Jekyll and Mr. Hyde.* Pasadena, California: Henry E. Huntington Library. Invaluable insights into the distortions which Mansfield helped popularize.

MCKAY, GEORGE L., ed. *The Stevenson Library of E. J. Beinecke.* VI vols. New Haven: Yale Library, 1951–1964. The catalogue of the most comprehensive Stevenson collection in the world. A necessary guide for anyone interested in Stevenson studies.

MIYOSHI, MASAO. "Dr. Jekyll and the Emergence of Mr. Hyde." *College English*, XXVII (March, 1966), 470–80.

MORRIS, DAVID B. *Robert Louis Stevenson and the Scottish Highlanders.* Sterling: Mackay, 1929. Contains historical information helpful in reading Stevenson's Scottish fiction.

Selected Bibliography

MYERS, F. W. Unpublished letters to Robert Louis Stevenson. Yale University: Beinecke Library. Letters on *Jekyll and Hyde* by the president of the Psychical Society.

OSBOURNE, KATHERINE DURHAM. *Robert Louis Stevenson in California.* Chicago: A. C. McClurg & Co., 1911. The suppressed version which revealed certain details in Stevenson's life which have only recently been verified.

RIEDEL, F. C. "A Classical Rhetorical Analysis of Some Elements of Stevenson's Essay Style." *Style,* 3, 182–99. Analyzes typical Stevenson passages in order to illustrate correspondence between sound and meaning. Finds Stevenson "a master craftsman who knew the tricks of his trade and did not hesitate to use them."

SCOTT, ANNE MACNICOL. "The Images of Light in Stevenson's *Weir of Hermiston.*" *English,* XIX (1970), 90–92. Suggests that light images convey the impressions presented by the main characters. "Stevenson had this sense of light as other people have a sense of timing . . . [and] he learned to use it faithfully as a subtle and unobtrusive gift."

SMITH, JANET ADAMS, ed. *Robert Louis Stevenson: Collected Poems.* London: Rupert Hart-Davis, 1952. The best and most authoritative collection of Stevenson's poems.

————. *Henry James and Robert Louis Stevenson: A Record of Friendship and Criticism.* London: Rupert Hart-Davis, 1948. Contains their correspondence as well as "The Age of Fiction" and "A Humble Remonstrance."

SNYDER, ALICE D. "Paradox and Antithesis in Stevenson's Essays: A Structural Study." *Journal of English and Germanic Philology,* XIV, 4 (October, 1920), 540–59. Fine study of Stevenson's essay structure.

SWINNERTON, FRANK. *Robert Louis Stevenson: A Critical Study.* New York: George H. Doran Co., 1923. Slightly revised second edition of the 1914 version. Still remains more a hatchet job than an objective analysis.

WARNER, FRED B., JR. "The Significance of Stevenson's 'Providence and the Guitar'." *English Literature in Transition,* XIV (1969), 103–14. Speculative reading in which he views the story as Stevenson's attempted justification of his affair with Fanny Osbourne.

WILSTACH, PAUL. *Richard Mansfield: The Man and the Actor.* New York: Scribners, 1909. Provides information on Mansfield's playing of the Jekyll-Hyde role.

2. General Background

BAIRD, JAMES. *Ishmael: A Study of the Symbolic Mode in Primitivism.* New York: Harper and Brothers, 1960. Guide to those writers who forsook their civilization for Oceania.

BENTLEY, ERIC. *The Life of the Drama*. New York: Atheneum, 1964. Especially valuable discussions of melodrama and farce.

CRAIG, DAVID. *Scottish Literature and the Scottish People 1680–1830*. London: Chatto and Windus, 1961. Survey of the social backgrounds of modern Scottish literature.

CRUSE, AMY. *The Victorians and Their Reading*. Boston: Houghton Mifflin, 1936. What every good Victorian library shelf should have had.

FRYE, NORTHROP. *The Anatomy of Criticism*. New York: Atheneum, 1966. Bible of archetypal criticism.

HOLLOWAY, JOHN. *The Victorian Sage*. New York: Norton, 1966. On the literary prophecy of the Victorian age.

HOUGHTON, WALTER. *The Victorian Frame of Mind*. New Haven: Yale University Press, 1957. Landmark in the writing of social history.

KINSLEY, JAMES. *Scottish Poetry: A Critical Survey*. London: Cassell, 1955. Comprehensive review of Scottish poetry. Especially fine on the modern period.

MARCUS, STEVEN. *The Other Victorians*. New York: Bantam Books, 1967. Investigation of Victorian underground literature and society.

MARTIN, BERNARD. *Ancient Mariner*. New York: Abingdon Press, 1960. Biography of John Newton upon whose exploits *Admiral Guinea* was partially based.

MIYOSHI, MASAO. *The Divided Self*. New York: New York University Press, 1969. First substantial investigation of duality in Victorian literature.

TYMMS, RALPH. *Doubles in Literary Psychology*. Cambridge, England: Bowes and Bowes, 1949. Catalogue of works in which doubles appear.

WATT, IAN. *The Rise of the Novel*. Berkeley: University of California Press, 1959. Study of the modern novel and the rise of Realism.

WITTIG, KURT. *The Scottish Tradition in Literature*. Edinburgh: Oliver and Boyd, 1958. Hurried view of Scottish literature; better on poetry than prose. Good introduction.

Index

Index